Georgina Ratnatunga in association
with Neil McPherson for the Finborough Theatre presents

Commemorating the 50th anniversary
of the death of artist Augustus John

Portraits

by William Douglas Home

T0347799

FINBOROUGH | THEATRE

First performance at the Finborough Theatre: Sunday, 7 August 2011

Portraits

by William Douglas Home

Cast in order of appearance

Joe	**Matt Barber**
Montgomery	**Hayward Morse**
Dorelia	**Kristin Milward**
Augustus John	**Peter Marinker**
George Bernard Shaw	**David Gooderson**
Matthew Smith	**Hayward Morse**
Cecil Beaton	**Hayward Morse**

Act One

Scene 1 | A Studio in Tite Street, Chelsea, London. Spring, 1944

Scene 2 | The same. Twenty-four hours later

Scene 3 | Fryern Court, Hampshire. October, 1944

Act Two

Scene 1 | Fryern Court, Hampshire. Spring, 1958

Scene 2 | The same. 1960

Scene 3 | The same. Some months later

There will be one interval of fifteen minutes

Director and Designer	**Alex Marker**
Lighting Designer	**Elliot Griggs**
Composer	**William Morris**
Sound Designer	**Edward Lewis**
Wardrobe Master	**Giles Chiplin**
Stage Manager	**Ben Karakashian**
Producer	**Georgina Ratnatunga**

Our patrons are respectfully reminded that, in this intimate theatre, any noise such as rustling programmes, talking or the ringing of mobile phones may distract the actors and your fellow audience-members.

Matt Barber | Joe

Trained at Bristol Old Vic Theatre School.

Theatre includes *You Can't Take it With You* (Southwark Playhouse), *Pygmalion* directed by Sir Peter Hall (The Old Vic, Theatre Royal Bath and International Tour), *Human by Default* (Old Red Lion Theatre), *Twelfth Night* (Birmingham Stage Company and International Tour), *The Misanthrope* (Bristol Old Vic) and *Edward II* (Rose Theatre, Bankside).

Film includes *Vivaldi* (Condor Pictures) and *The Alchemistic Suitcase* (B Good Pictures).

Television includes *The Heart of Thomas Hardy* and *Being Human* (BBC) and *S' N' M' – The British Dream*.

David Gooderson | George Bernard Shaw

At the Finborough Theatre, David wrote and directed *The Killing of Mr Toad* (2009), and appeared in *The Potting Shed* (2010 and 2011).

Theatre includes *Saint's Day*, *The Neighbours*, *Overboard*, *The Simpleton of the Unexpected Isles*, *A Penny for a Song* (Orange Tree Theatre, Richmond), *A Midsummer Night's Dream*, *Ariadne on Naxos*, *Die Fledermaus* (English Touring Opera), *The Taming of the Shrew*, *Richard III*, *King Lear* (Ludlow Festival), *A Midsummer Night's Dream*, *Macbeth*, *The Boys from Syracuse*, *Lady Be Good* and *The Taming of the Shrew* (Open Air Theatre, Regent's Park).

Film includes *Limited Edition*.

Television includes *Doctors*, *A Touch of Frost*, *Casualty*, *Footballer's Wives*, *Hidden City*, *Searching*, *Just William*, *Rumpole*, *Murder Most Horrid*, *Lovejoy*, *Bluebell*, *Dr Who* and *Seaview*.

Writing includes *The Wind in the Willows* (West End), *Walk or Die*, *Waste of Glory*, *Death of a Village* and *So Great a Crime* (all BBC Radio Four).

Peter Marinker | Augustus John

At the Finborough Theatre, Peter has appeared in *The Early Hours of a Reviled Man* (1999), The Godot Company's *Waiting for Godot* (2003) and *Hurried Steps* (2009).

Theatre includes *Southwark Mysteries* (Shakespeare's Globe), *The Curse of the Starving Class* (Royal Shakespeare Company), *The Iceman Cometh* (Lyric Theatre, Belfast), *Are You Lonesome Tonight?* (Phoenix Theatre), *The Merchant of Venice* (The Old Vic), Beckett's *A Piece of Monologue* (Traverse Theatre, Edinburgh and recording for Naxos Audio Books). With Howard Barker's company The Wrestling School, he appeared in *Seduction of Almighty God* and *Hurts Given and Received* (Riverside Studios).

Film and Television includes *Lifetime* (Galway Festival 2011), *United 93*, *Love Actually*, *Event Horizon*, *Judge Dredd*, *Russia House*, *The Emerald Forest*, *Enemy Mine*, *Martian Chronicles*, *Fear is the Key*, *Family*, *The Vice*, *Doctors*, *Bodyguards*, *Young Indie* and *Casualty*. He was Dialogue Director for John Boorman on *The Emerald Forest* and *The Tailor of Panama*, and for Wolfgang Petersen on *Das Boot* and *Enemy Mine*.

He is a co-founder of The Godot Company, director of the Bookshop Theatre Company and a member of The People Show.

Kristin Milward | Dorelia

At the Finborough Theatre, Kristin has appeared in *The Women of Troy* (1991), *Child of the Forest* (2000), *Natural Inclinations* (2002), *I Wish to Die Singing* (2005) and *Love Child* (2007).

Theatre includes *Huis Clos* (King's Head Theatre), *The Illustrious Corpse* (Soho Theatre), *Women of Troy* (Orange Tree Theatre, Richmond), *Soap Opera* (The Caird Company), *The Snow Palace* (Sphinx Theatre and Tricycle Theatre), *Wounds to the Face* (National Tour for The Wrestling School), *Uncle Vanya* (The Wrestling School), *The Bitter Tears of Petra Von Kant* (Latchmere Theatre), *La Chunga* (Old Red Lion Theatre), *Les Liaisons Dangereuses* (Royal Shakespeare Company, West End and Broadway), *Burleigh Grimes* (Bridewell Theatre) and *The Chance* (Belfast Festival).

Film includes *Arabs in London* (EBLA International Film) and *Freestyle* (Film London Microwave). She has just finished two films shot in Norway – *The End of Winter* and *For the Love of Him* to be released in 2011.

Television includes *New Tricks*, *Poppyland*, *To the Lighthouse* and *EastEnders* (all BBC).

Hayward Morse | Montgomery / Matthew Smith / Cecil Beaton

At the Finborough Theatre, Hayward has appeared in *Eden's Empire* (2006), *Weapons of Happiness* (2008) and *A Day by the Sea* (2008). Trained at RADA.

Theatre includes the original production of *What the Butler Saw* (Queen's Theatre), *Butley* (Morosco Theatre, New York City) where he received a Tony Award nomination, the original production of *The Rocky Horror Show* (King's Road Theatre), *Travels With My Aunt* (National Tour and English Theatre, Vienna), *The Hound of the Baskervilles* (Gawsworth Hall), *The School for Wives* (Upstairs at the Gatehouse) and *The Spanish Tragedy* (Rose Theatre, Bankside).

Film includes *Tam Lynn, Agency, Death Wish 3* and *The Scared of Death Society*.

Television includes *Footballers Wives* and *James May's Manlab*.

Radio includes Lester Nicholson in *The Archers*. He has also recorded over a hundred unabridged audiobooks.

William Douglas Home | Playwright

Douglas Home was the third son of the 13th Earl of Home and Lady Lilian Lambton, daughter of Frederick Lambton, 4th Earl of Durham. His oldest brother was Sir Alec Douglas Home who was Prime Minister from 1963 to 1964. He was educated at Eton College and New College, Oxford where he read History. His first play, *Murder in Pupil Room*, was performed by his classmates at Eton in 1926 when he was only fourteen. During the Second World War, Douglas Home was an officer in the 141st Regiment, Royal Armoured Corps (The Buffs). He was court-martialed and imprisoned during the Second World War for his refusal to obey orders during the Allied operation to capture the port of Le Havre in September 1944 because French civilians had not been permitted to evacuate. He went on to become one of the West End's most successful post-war dramatists with plays including *Now Barabbas* (1947), *The Chiltern Hundreds* (1947), *The Thistle and the Rose* (1948), *The Reluctant Debutante* (1955) (which was twice filmed, most recently in 2003 under the title *What a Girl Wants*, starring Colin Firth and Kelly Preston), *The Reluctant Peer* (1964), *Betzi* (1965), *A Friend Indeed* (1965), *The Secretary Bird* (1967), *The Queen's Highland Servant* (1967), *The Jockey Club Stakes* (1970), *Lloyd George Knew My Father* (1972), *At the End of the Day* (1973), *The Dame of Sark* (1974), *The Kingfisher* (1978) and *After the Ball is Over* (1985). *Portraits* was originally performed at the Malvern Festival in May 1987 in a production directed by John Dexter, and transferred to the Savoy Theatre, London, on 11 August 1987. William Douglas Home died in 1992.

Alex Marker | Director and Designer

Alex Marker has been Resident Designer of the Finborough Theatre since 2002 where his designs have included *Charlie's Wake, The Women's War, How I Got That Story, Soldiers, Happy Family, Trelawny of the 'Wells', Hortensia and the Museum of Dreams, Albert's Boy, Lark Rise To Candleford, Red Night, The Representative, Eden's Empire, Love Child, Little Madam, Plague Over England,* and its West End transfer to the Duchess Theatre, *Hangover Square, Sons of York, Untitled, Painting A Wall, Death of Long Pig, Molière or The League of Hypocrites, Dream of the Dog* and its West End transfer to the Trafalgar Studios and *Me and Juliet.*

Previous directing includes a staged reading of Iain Finlay MacLeod's *Atman,* starring Jasper Britton and Alan Cox, as part of *Vibrant – An Anniversary Festival of Finborough Playwrights* (2010). Trained in Theatre Design at Wimbledon School of Art, he has designed over fifty productions including *King Arthur* (Arcola Theatre), *The Schools' Theatre Festival* (Young Vic), *Jus' Like That! A Night Out With Tommy Cooper* (UK Tour), *My Real War 1914-?* (Trafalgar Studios and National Tour), *An Eligible Man* (New End Theatre, Hampstead), *The Viewing Room* (Arts Theatre), *Sweet Charity* (Theatre Royal, Drury Lane), *The Pink Bedroom* (Courtyard Theatre), *Oklahoma!* (New Wimbledon Theatre) and *Cooking With Elvis* (Lyceum Theatre, Crewe). His work has been extensively featured in exhibitions, most recently as part of the *Transformation and Revelation: UK Design for Performance* in Cardiff.

He is also Director of the Questors Youth Theatre, the largest youth theatre in London.

Elliot Griggs | Lighting Designer

At the Finborough Theatre, Elliot was Lighting Designer for *And I And Silence* (2011) and *Northern Star* (2011).

Trained in Lighting Design at Royal Academy of Dramatic Art. Lighting Designs include *dirty butterfly, Nocturnal* and *Our Town* (RADA), *Drift: Photo 51* (Edinburgh Academy), *The Lady's Not For Burning, West Side Story, 'Tis Pity She's a Whore* and *Macbeth* (Warwick Arts Centre), *Much Ado About Nothing* (Belgrade Theatre), *By The Bog of Cats* (National Student Drama Festival 2010), *Dido and Aeneas* (St. Paul's Church and Tour) and *Elephant's Graveyard* (National Student Drama Festival 2009) for which he was awarded the ShowLight award for Lighting Design. Assistant Lighting Designs include *The Young Idea* (RADA) for Natasha Chivers.

William Morris | Composer

A composer, musical director, educator and performer, William was the inaugural Director of Music for the British Humanist Association, composing music for ceremonies and public occasions. He founded the British Humanist Association Choir which performs his music at high profile events such as *Nine Lessons* and *Carols for Godless People* in Bloomsbury Theatre and was featured on BBC news and radio. William's collaboration with writer Susan Pleat began in 2010 with the musical *Gouache and the Night Sky*. His collaboration with Simon Warne includes the musicals *The Two Hermiones* (Electric Theatre, Guildford), *Rasputin* (Musical Futures at Greenwich Theatre), *Stratford Street* (ANMT, Chicago and Los Angeles, and King's Head Theatre) and *What You Will* (Hampton Hill Playhouse). His commissions across a variety of media include the ballet film *Facing Mara* (Native Voice Films), the BBC Radio play *The Glass Case*, and more recently the critically acclaimed More4 documentary *On That Day*. He also has a new choral commission being performed in November as part of the 2011 Kingston Festival of the Voice at the Chapel Royal, Hampton Court.

Edward Lewis | Sound Designer

At the Finborough Theatre, Edward was Sound Designer *for Vibrant – An Anniversary Festival of Finborough Playwrights* (2010), *In The Blood* (2010), *The December Man/L'homme de Décembre* (2011), *Accolade* (2011), *Bed and Sofa* (2011) and *Beating Heart Cadaver* (2011).

Studied Music at Oxford University and subsequently trained as a composer and sound designer at the Bournemouth Media School. Theatre includes *On The Rocks*, *Amongst Friends*, *Darker Shores* (Hampstead Theatre), *Slowly*, *Hurts Given and Received*, *Apple Pie* (Riverside Studios), *Measure for Measure* (Sherman Cymru), *Emo* (Bristol Old Vic and Young Vic), *I Am Falling* (Sadler's Wells and Gate Theatre), *The Stronger*, *The Pariah*, *Boy With A Suitcase*, *Le Marriage and Meetings* (Arcola Theatre), *Hedda*, *Breathing Irregular* (Gate Theatre), *Madness in Valencia* (Trafalgar Studios), *The Madness of George III* (National Tour), *Love*, *Question Mark* (New Diorama Theatre), *Knives In Hens* (BAC), *Personal Enemy* (White Bear Theatre Club and US Tour), *Kalagora* (National and International Tour), *Mad*, *Funny*, *Just*, *Mimi And The Stalker* (Theatre

503), *The London Plays* (Old Red Lion Theatre), *Cyrano De Bergerac*, *Bloody Poetry* and *Madman's Confession* (White Bear Theatre Club), *No Way Out* (Hen and Chickens Theatre), *Striking 12* (Waterloo East Theatre), *Heat and Light* (Hampstead Theatre), *Diary of A Madman* (Rosemary Branch Theatre), *The Death Of Cool* (Tristan Bates Theatre) and *Full Circle* (Oval House Theatre), as well as on the Arden Project for the Old Vic. He has recently been nominated for an Off West End Theatre Award, and films he has recently worked on have won several awards at the LA and Filmstock International Film Festivals.

Georgina Ratnatunga | Producer
At the Finborough Theatre, Georgina was General Manager during 2011. Producing includes *The Caucasian Chalk Circle* (Edinburgh Festival and The Wirksworth Festival) and *Road* (TC's, Birmingham). She is Assistant Director at Theatre Studio West. As Production Co-ordinator, she is currently working on a series of short Harold Pinter plays which are touring around Europe in autumn 2011.

FINBOROUGH | THEATRE

Fringe Theatre of the Year 2010

STAGE 100 AWARDS

Winner – *London Theatre Reviews'* Empty Space Peter Brook Award 2010

"One of the most stimulating venues in London, fielding a programme that is a bold mix of trenchant, politically thought-provoking new drama and shrewdly chosen revivals of neglected works from the past." *The Independent*

"A disproportionately valuable component of the London theatre ecology. Its programme combines new writing and revivals, in selections intelligent and audacious." *Financial Times*

"A blazing beacon of intelligent endeavour, nurturing new writers while finding and reviving neglected curiosities from home and abroad."
The Daily Telegraph

Founded in 1980, the multi-award-winning Finborough Theatre presents plays and music theatre, concentrated exclusively on new writing and genuine 'rediscoveries' from the 19th and 20th centuries. We offer a stimulating and inclusive programme, appealing to theatregoers of all generations and from a broad spectrum of the population. Behind the scenes, we continue to discover and develop a new generation of theatre makers – through our vibrant Literary Department, our internship programme, our Resident Assistant Director Programme, and our partnership with the National Theatre Studio – the Leverhulme Bursary for Emerging Directors.

Despite remaining completely unfunded, the Finborough Theatre has an unparalleled track record of attracting the finest creative talent to work with us, as well as discovering new playwrights who go on to become leading voices in British theatre. Under Artistic Director Neil McPherson, it has discovered some of the UK's most exciting new playwrights including Laura Wade, James Graham, Mike Bartlett, Sarah Grochala, Jack Thorne, Simon Vinnicombe, Alexandra Wood, Al Smith, Nicholas de Jongh and Anders Lustgarten.

Artists working at the theatre in the 1980s included Clive Barker, Rory Bremner, Nica Burns, Kathy Burke, Ken Campbell, Jane Horrocks and Claire Dowie. In the 1990s, the Finborough Theatre became known for new writing including Naomi Wallace's first play *The War Boys*; Rachel Weisz in David Farr's *Neville Southall's Washbag*; four plays by Anthony

Neilson including *Penetrator* and *The Censor*, both of which transferred to the Royal Court Theatre; and new plays by Tony Marchant, David Eldridge, Mark Ravenhill and Phil Willmott. New writing development included a number of works that went to become modern classics including Mark Ravenhill's *Shopping and F***king*, Conor McPherson's *This Lime Tree Bower*, Naomi Wallace's *Slaughter City* and Martin McDonagh's *The Pillowman*.

Since 2000, new British plays have included Laura Wade's London debut *Young Emma*, commissioned by the Finborough Theatre; James Graham's *Albert's Boy* with Victor Spinetti; Sarah Grochala's *S27*; Peter Nichols' *Lingua Franca*, which transferred Off-Broadway; Anders Lustgarten's *A Day at the Racists* which won the Catherine Johnson Best Play Award and the Harold Pinter Playwrights' Award; and Joy Wilkinson's *Fair*; Nicholas de Jongh's *Plague Over England*; and Jack Thorne's *Fanny and Faggot*, all of which transferred to the West End. The late Miriam Karlin made her last stage appearance in *Many Roads to Paradise* in 2008. Many of our new plays have been published and are on sale from our website.

UK premieres of foreign plays have included Brad Fraser's *Wolfboy*; Lanford Wilson's *Sympathetic Magic*; Larry Kramer's *The Destiny of Me*; Tennessee Williams' *Something Cloudy, Something Clear*; the English premiere of Robert McLellan's Scots language classic, *Jamie the Saxt*; and three West End transfers – Frank McGuinness' *Gates of Gold* with William Gaunt and John Bennett, Joe DiPietro's *F***ing Men* and Craig Higginson's *Dream of the Dog* with Janet Suzman.

Rediscoveries of neglected work have included the first London revivals of Rolf Hochhuth's *Soldiers* and *The Representative*; Keith Dewhurst's *Lark Rise to Candleford*; *The Women's War*, an evening of original suffragette plays; *Etta Jenks* with Clarke Peters and Daniela Nardini; Noël Coward's first play, *The Rat Trap*; Charles Wood's *Jingo* with Susannah Harker; two sell out productions by J.M. Barrie – *What Every Woman Knows* and *Quality Street*; and Emlyn Williams' *Accolade*.

Music Theatre has included the new (premieres from Grant Olding, Charles Miller, Michael John LaChuisa, Adam Guettel, Andrew Lippa and Adam Gwon's *Ordinary Days* which transferred to the West End) and the old (the UK premiere of Rodgers and Hammerstein's *State Fair* which also transferred to the West End, and the acclaimed Celebrating British Music Theatre series, reviving forgotten British musicals).

The Finborough Theatre won *London Theatre Reviews'* Empty Space Peter Brook Award in 2010, the Empty Space Peter Brook Award's Dan Crawford Pub Theatre Award in 2005 and 2008, the Empty Space Peter Brook Mark Marvin Award in 2004, and four awards at the inaugural 2011 Off West End Awards. It is the only theatre without public funding to be awarded the Pearson Playwriting Award bursary for writers Chris Lee in 2000, Laura Wade in 2005 (who also went on to win the Critics' Circle Theatre Award for Most Promising Playwright, the George Devine Award and an Olivier Award nomination), for James Graham in 2006, for Al Smith in 2007, for Anders Lustgarten in 2009 and Simon Vinnicombe in 2010. Three bursary holders (Laura Wade, James Graham and Anders Lustgarten) have also won the Catherine Johnson Award for Best Play written by a bursary holder. Artistic Director Neil McPherson has won two Best Artistic Director awards including the Off West End Award in 2011, and a Writers' Guild Award for the Encouragement of New Writing.

www.finboroughtheatre.co.uk

FINBOROUGH | THEATRE

118 Finborough Road, London SW10 9ED
admin@finboroughtheatre.co.uk
www.finboroughtheatre.co.uk

Supported by

The Leverhulme Bursary for Emerging Directors is a partnership between the National Theatre Studio and the Finborough Theatre, supported by The Leverhulme Trust.

Ecovenue is a European Regional Development Fund backed three year initiative of The Theatres Trust, aiming to improve the environmental sustainability of 48 small to medium sized performing arts spaces across London. www.ecovenue.org.uk

The Finborough Theatre is a member of the Independent Theatre Council, Musical Theatre Matters UK (MTM:UK) and The Earl's Court Society www.earlscourtsociety.org.uk

The Finborough Wine Café
Contact Rob Malcolm or Monique Ziervogel on 020 7373 0745 or finboroughwinecafe@gmail.com

Online
Join us at Facebook, Twitter, MySpace and YouTube.

Mailing

Email admin@finboroughtheatre.co.uk or give your details to our Box Office staff to join our free email list. If you would like to be sent a free season leaflet every three months, just include your postal address and postcode.

Feedback

We welcome your comments, complaints and suggestions. Write to Finborough Theatre, 118 Finborough Road, London SW10 9ED or email us at admin@finboroughtheatre.co.uk

Friends

The Finborough Theatre is a registered charity. We receive no public funding, and rely solely on the support of our audiences. Please do consider supporting us by becoming a member of our Friends of the Finborough Theatre scheme. There are four categories of Friends, each offering a wide range of benefits.

Brandon Thomas Friends – Bruce Cleave. Mike Lewendon.

Richard Tauber Friends – Harry MacAuslan. Brian Smith.

Lionel Monckton Friends – Bridget MacDougall.

William Terriss Friends – Leo and Janet Liebster. Philip Hooker. Peter Lobl. Bhagat Sharma. Thurloe and Lyndhurst LLP. Jon Sedmak.

Smoking is not permitted in the auditorium and the use of cameras and recording equipment is strictly prohibited.

In accordance with the requirements of the Royal Borough of Kensington and Chelsea:

1. The public may leave at the end of the performance by all doors and such doors must at that time be kept open.
2. All gangways, corridors, staircases and external passageways intended for exit shall be left entirely free from obstruction whether permanent or temporary.
3. Persons shall not be permitted to stand or sit in any of the gangways intercepting the seating or to sit in any of the other gangways.

The Finborough Theatre is licensed by the Royal Borough of Kensington and Chelsea to The Steam Industry, a registered charity and a company limited by guarantee. Registered in England no. 3448268. Registered Charity no. 1071304. Registered Office: 118 Finborough Road, London SW10 9ED. The Steam Industry is under the Artistic Direction of Phil Willmott. www.philwillmott.co.uk

Portraits

Production Acknowledgements

Assistant Stage Manager	**Rhian Morris**
Deputy Stage Manager	**Russell Bailey**
Poster and Leaflet Design	**Rebecca Maltby**
Wardrobe Consultants	**Sarah Andrews**
	Jennie Yates
Construction	**Philip Lindley**
	Ellis McNorthey-Gibbs
Rehearsal Space	**The Questors Theatre**
Special Thanks	**Elaine Alderson**
	Theresa Byrne
	Claire Evans
	Kingston College
	Nigel Lewis
	Geoffrey Morgan
	Alan N Smith
	Liorah Tchiprout

William Douglas Home

PORTRAITS

OBERON BOOKS
LONDON

WWW.OBERONBOOKS.COM

Trade edition first published in 2011 by Oberon Books Ltd.
521 Caledonian Road, London N7 9RH
Tel: +44 (0) 20 7607 3637 / Fax: +44 (0) 20 7607 3629
info@oberonbooks.com
www.oberonbooks.com

A catalogue record for this book is available from the British
Library.

ISBN: 978-1-84943-210-8

Cover design by Sasha Marrek.

Printed in Great Britain by CPI Antony Rowe, Chippenham.

Characters

JOE, a young Guards' Colonel

MONTGOMERY

DORELIA

AUGUSTUS JOHN

G.B.S.

MATTHEW SMITH

CECIL BEATON

The author wishes to record the deep impression made on him by reading Michael Holroyd's definitive biography of Augustus John.

ACT I

Scene 1
A Studio in Tite Street, Chelsea, London. Spring, 1944

Scene 2
The same. Twenty-four hours later

Scene 3
Fryern Court, Hampshire. October, 1944

ACT II

Scene 1
Fryern Court, Hampshire. Spring, 1958

Scene 2
The same. 1960

Scene 3
The same. Some months later

Portraits was first presented at the Malvern Festival in May, 1987. The play was subsequently presented at the Savoy Theatre, London, on 11th August, 1987, by arrangement with Hugh Wontner, by Duncan C. Weldon and Jerome Minskoff for Triumph Theatre Productions Ltd. and Riggs O'Hara in association with Brad and Patty Griffiths for the New Theatre Company Ltd., with the following cast of characters:

JOE, Stephen Boxer
THE SUBJECTS, Simon Ward
DORELIA, Pamela Lane
AUGUSTUS, Keith Michell
G.B.S., Richard Wordsworth

Directed by John Dexter
Designed by Brien Vahey

PROLOGUE

A young Guards' Colonel enters upstage and comes downstage. He looks at his watch. He looks to the prompt corner. He moves upstage and looks off. He returns to his position downstage.

An actor enters, running, and crosses to the COLONEL.

They shake hands.

COLONEL: (*To the audience.*) Good-evening, my name is (*Actor's name.*), and I'm playing Montgomery's staff officer. This is (*Actor's name.*), and he's playing Monty, or at least as near as he can get to him. Later on he will also play Matthew Smith* and Cecil Beaton*. (*Actress's name.*) is playing Dorelia. (*Actor's name.*) is playing George Bernard Shaw. And finally, (*Actor's name.*) is playing … Augustus John.

* In the original London production, Simon Ward played the parts of MONTY, MATTHEW SMITH and CECIL BEATON. However, it is not essential that one actor plays the subjects. If preferred, each part may be played by a separate actor.

ACT I

SCENE I

A studio in Tite Street, Chelsea, London. Spring, 1944.

When the CURTAIN rises MONTGOMERY, wearing his well-known beret with two badges, is moving round, inspecting the contents of the studio – the pictures on the walls and on the floor, the furniture. The young Guards' COLONEL stands there watching him.

MONTY: (*Halting in his promenade, addressing the Colonel.*) How much longer is this fellow going to keep us waiting?

COLONEL: He'll be here any moment, sir, I'm sure.

MONTY: What time was the appointment made for?

COLONEL: Ten fifteen, sir.

MONTY: (*Looking at his watch.*) Well, it's ten sixteen now. (*He resumes his pacing. He picks up a dirty glass and puts it down and then runs a finger down a piece of furniture and notes the dust thereon. Holding up his dirty finger.*) Look at that! He's late, he's dirty and he drinks. And there are women in it somewhere.

COLONEL: You're dead on target, sir, as usual.

MONTY: What's the name again?

COLONEL: John, sir.

MONTY: John what?

COLONEL: John nothing, sir. His name's Augustus John. And John's the surname.

MONTY: There's a fellow in the Navy called John, with a fancy name.

COLONEL: That's right, sir. Caspar. He's his son.

MONTY: Poor fellow. He's a captain, isn't he?

COLONEL: That's right, sir.

MONTY: I don't know which this room smells of worst, drink or tobacco.

COLONEL: He's a first-class artist, sir. He got the OM for it recently.

MONTY: I can't see why.

COLONEL: Well, look at that, sir. (*He points at a picture on the wall of the studio.*)

MONTY: I am looking at it.

COLONEL: Well, it's good, sir, isn't it?

MONTY: It's not by him … Unless he signs himself Gwen!

COLONEL: Sorry my mistake, sir. That's his sister.

MONTY: Was that her who let us in?

COLONEL: No, sir. She's dead.

MONTY: Well, who's the woman?

COLONEL: She's Dorelia. She's famous.

MONTY: What for?

COLONEL: Well, she's been the model for a lot of his best pictures.

MONTY: Since when?

COLONEL: Since his wife died, sir, if not before.

MONTY: When did his wife die?

COLONEL: Years ago, sir. Quite a bit before the first war.

MONTY: Have you done a course on John or something?

COLONEL: No, sir. I was taught about him at school.

MONTY: He's as good as that, then, is he?

COLONEL: Better, sir. He's probably our greatest artist.

MONTY: That's what the art master told you, is it?

COLONEL: Yes, sir.

MONTY: What else did he tell you?

COLONEL: That he broke his first wife's heart.

MONTY: Is that authenticated?

COLONEL: Don't ask me, sir. The art master said he was a womanizer and he always had been.

MONTY: What was she called?

COLONEL: Ida – Ida Nettleship.

MONTY: And what was she like?

COLONEL: The art master told us that she was the perfect wife for somebody who didn't want one.

MONTY: Poor girl! Why did she die so young?

COLONEL: After childbirth, sir.

MONTY: (*Jerking a thumb towards the door.*) Then he picked up this woman?

COLONEL: He'd picked her up already, sir. According to the art master Dorelia and Ida and Augustus were great friends.

MONTY: A *ménage à trois*, you mean.

COLONEL: That's a fairly modest estimate, I'd say, sir, when you take in all his other mistresses and models.

MONTY: Quite a harem, eh?

COLONEL: Oh, yes, sir, over the years.

MONTY: And you learned all this from the art master at school, did you?

COLONEL: Yes, sir.

MONTY: And you've not forgotten it?

COLONEL: No, sir.

MONTY: Why not?

COLONEL: Because I found it fascinating, sir.

MONTY: Why?

COLONEL: Why not, sir?

MONTY: Because you want to be an artist or because you want to be a lecher when this war is over?

COLONEL: I'd like to be an artist, sir.

MONTY: And not a lecher?

COLONEL: No, sir.

MONTY: Well, you may not find it easy. Artists live on the excuse that they must have a free hand or they can't paint. And, from what I've seen of you I'd say you were a steady and straightforward fellow with a pretty wife and pretty little daughter. And from that I would deduce you wouldn't want a free hand. So you'd better cut the artist out and stick to soldiering. And finish up a general like me! How would you like that?

COLONEL: Not much, sir.

MONTY: So you'd rather be an artist.

COLONEL: Yes, sir.

MONTY: You'd rather be Augustus John than me, in fact.

COLONEL: I'm sorry. But I would, sir.

MONTY: Don't be sorry. *Chacun à son goût.* And anyway it's your loss not mine. That's the second time I've talked French in the last five minutes. I must be instinctively rehearsing for the big push. Accent all right?

COLONEL: *Bien, monsieur!*

MONTY: Don't be cheeky. Well, I'll let you paint me when this war is over, if we both survive.

COLONEL: Thanks very much, sir.

MONTY: Are you looking forward to it?

COLONEL: What? To painting you, sir?

MONTY: No, the Second Front.

COLONEL: Like mad, sir.

MONTY: (*Probing.*) Even though you'd rather be Augustus John than me?

DORELIA comes in before the COLONEL can answer. She has already met them at the front door.

DORELIA: Augustus won't be long. Do sit down somewhere.

MONTY: I prefer to stand.

COLONEL: We've done a lot of sitting in the staff car. All the way from –

MONTY: (*Cutting in.*) Careless talk costs lives, Joe.

COLONEL: Sorry, sir.

DORELIA: (*To the COLONEL.*) Do smoke if you'd like to. I'm afraid I've got no cigarettes.

MONTY: He doesn't smoke when he's with me.

COLONEL: That's right.

MONTY: He's just been telling me that you're the model for a lot of famous pictures. I've not seen them, I'm afraid.

COLONEL: Well, you've missed something, sir. They're beautiful. Well that goes without saying, doesn't it?

DORELIA: No longer, Colonel, I'm afraid. The model isn't what she used to be.

COLONEL: I wouldn't say that.

DORELIA: You're too polite to, that's why.

MONTY: Are you still his model?

DORELIA: Sometimes – when he can't find someone younger, General. But that's not very often.

MONTY: Have you always been his model?

DORELIA: Ever since I can remember. Well, that's not quite true. Of course, I can remember things before that. I typed in an office, General, would you believe that, when I was a young girl.

MONTY: If you say so – yes.

DORELIA: And then I went to art school in the evenings. And I met Augustus there. And fell in love with him.

MONTY: You didn't marry him though?

DORELIA: No.

MONTY: Because he was already married.

DORELIA: Yes. To Ida. (*Pointing at a picture or a sketch on the wall.*) That's her.

MONTY: By his sister, Gwen. Who's dead.

DORELIA: That's right. She died in France in nineteen thirty-nine. In Dieppe on her way home. She was lying in the street with very little money on her – and she died in hospital. Like Ida had before her, when she had her last child. And I loved them both. As much as I loved him.

COLONEL: And which is the best artist, do you think. Gwen or Augustus?

DORELIA: (*Smiling.*) You tell me!

COLONEL: You can't compare them. They're both so different.

DORELIA: You're very tactful.

MONTY: That's why I employ him on my staff. And as he's fond of pictures I brought him along.

DORELIA: (*To the COLONEL.*) Are you a painter yourself?

COLONEL: Well, I dabble.

DORELIA: What at?

COLONEL: Landscapes – women – wife and daughter for example.

DORELIA: Good for you.

MONTY: I paint too.

DORELIA: I was going to ask you, General.

MONTY: Yes. Not my wife though. She's dead. And I haven't got a daughter. Just a son who won't sit still. And so I stick to landscapes.

COLONEL: And they're damned good – let me tell you.

MONTY: You'd better! (*To DORELIA.*) He knows if he doesn't say that he'll get a posting.

DORELIA: What does that mean?

COLONEL: It means he'll post me.

DORELIA: Post you! Where to?

MONTY: The most unattractive place that I can think of.

DORELIA: Would you really, General?

MONTY: I wouldn't put it past me.

DORELIA: Poor man.

MONTY: (*Softening.*) Do you mind if he smokes?

DORELIA: No, of course not.

MONTY: Go and do it over there then.

COLONEL: Thank you, sir. (*He retires to the other end of the studio.*)

MONTY: And don't set fire to yourself – or the billet.

COLONEL: I'll try not to, sir.

DORELIA: I do hope that Augustus hasn't gone back to bed. Should I go and see?

MONTY: Don't bother. I'm enjoying myself. What year did you first meet John?

DORELIA: I'm very vague about dates.

MONTY: How old were you?

DORELIA: Twenty-two.

MONTY: And you became his model?

DORELIA: That's right.

MONTY: When his wife died?

DORELIA: You do ask a lot of questions. No, before. Before the first war.

MONTY: And you say you loved her?

DORELIA: Yes.

MONTY: And did she love you?

DORELIA: Yes. She did.

MONTY: She didn't mind then?

DORELIA: Mind what?

MONTY: You being his model?

DORELIA: Heavens no. Why should she? Oh dear, I'm afraid I'm shocking you!

MONTY: (*Pointing to the COLONEL.*) You're shocking him too!

DORELIA: Am I? I'm so sorry.

COLONEL: Not so you'd notice!

DORELIA: Well, she did mind, I suppose. What woman wouldn't. Just as I mind when he has some pretty young girl as a model now. She rose above it, though.

MONTY: Like you do?

DORELIA: Like I try to.

MONTY: And she died in childbirth?

DORELIA: After her fifth baby.

MONTY: My wife only had one. She's dead too.

DORELIA: I'm sorry.

MONTY: That's all right. And was the baby all right?

DORELIA: Quite all right.

MONTY: Good – so was mine. I called it David.

DORELIA: Ida called her first son that.

MONTY: Wise girl.

DORELIA: I called mine Pyramus. What do you think of that?

MONTY: It's not as bad as Bernard.

DORELIA: You're called Bernard, aren't you, General?

MONTY: That's right.

DORELIA: And you don't like it?

MONTY: Not much.

DORELIA: I do. It reminds me of those great big dogs who dig up snow-bound travellers and give them brandy.

The COLONEL turns away and smiles.

MONTY: What's the joke, Joe?

COLONEL: I was visualizing you, sir, climbing up the Eiger carrying a water-bottle.

MONTY: Very funny. He's a bit of a wag is my colonel.

DORELIA: Good for him. Life wouldn't be supportable without them, would it?

MONTY: So they tell me. What's the naval fellow's name, Joe?

COLONEL: Caspar, sir.

MONTY: (*To DORELIA.*) Is he yours?

DORELIA: No, he's Ida's. He's a captain now, you know. Not very high, I know, compared with you – but something.

MONTY: Captains in the Navy are equivalent to colonels in the Army.

DORELIA: Oh, I didn't know that.

MONTY: So he's done as well as Joe has.

DORELIA: He's much older.

MONTY: How old is he?

DORELIA: Forty something. (*To the* COLONEL.) How old are you?

COLONEL: Twenty something!

MONTY: Wise man – he's not telling!

DORELIA: You're very young to be a colonel, aren't you?

MONTY: Too young. You're quite right, madam. Far too young. He did so well at Alamein we couldn't keep him down, though.

DORELIA: And you look so gentle.

COLONEL: What about your own son? Is he in the Services?

DORELIA: One is, yes. But not Pyramus. He died when he was eight. From meningitis.

MONTY: I'm so sorry.

DORELIA: Thank you. He was beautiful. Too beautiful to live. That sounds a silly thing to say. But it can be true, can't it?

MONTY: Certainly it can.

DORELIA: You're thinking of your wife.

MONTY: Yes – among others.

DORELIA: There're so many, aren't there?

COLONEL: Rupert Brooke for instance.

DORELIA: That's right, Rupert.

COLONEL: Did you know him?

DORELIA: Slightly. He was beautiful – like Pyramus.

MONTY: "If I should die … " how does it go, Joe?

COLONEL: All of it, sir?

MONTY: I'll stop you if you overdo it.

COLONEL: (*To DORELIA.*) Do you mind?

DORELIA: Mind? No, I like it.

COLONEL: So do I – it's a bit too well-known though, isn't it, like Shakespeare, chock full of quotations.

MONTY: Get on with it, man.

COLONEL: You've made me nervous now, sir. So I'm sure to make a mess of it.

MONTY: All right then. I'll do it.

COLONEL: No, sir. You don't know it.

MONTY: Nonsense – I know every word.

COLONEL: No, sir. You don't. You always paraphrase it. And that kills it stone dead. Sorry, sir, but someone's got to tell you, so it may as well be me, as no one else would dare to.

MONTY: (*To DORELIA.*) Well, what do you think of that? Rank insubordination!

DORELIA: I think he deserves a medal.

MONTY: Well, he won't get it from me, unless he carries out my orders.

COLONEL: OK, sir. You've asked for it!

MONTY: And cut the paraphrasing out!

COLONEL: (*Reciting beautifully.*)

"If I should die, think only this of me:
That there's some corner of a foreign field
That is forever England. There shall be
In that rich earth a richer dust" –

AUGUSTUS JOHN comes in, dressed in a brown smock, open shirt and scarf and sandals.

The COLONEL breaks off.

AUGUSTUS: Don't mind me, carry on.

COLONEL: No, sir. I was just filling in the time.

AUGUSTUS: Sorry I'm late. (*He shakes hands with* MONTY.)

MONTY: That's all right, we've been talking.

AUGUSTUS: (*Looking at the* COLONEL.) Who's this?

MONTY: He's on my staff.

AUGUSTUS: (*To the* COLONEL.) I'd like to paint you, young man.

MONTY: Well, you can't. You're painting me.

AUGUSTUS: You wouldn't like him on your knee?

MONTY: No, I would not.

AUGUSTUS gives MONTY a long stare.

DORELIA slips away.

AUGUSTUS: (*Finally.*) You're no oil painting, are you – as the saying goes. Still, we'll have to see what we can do. Sit down there, will you.

He leads him to the chair, sits him down and moves away to look at him.

Not so stiff. Relax. (*He busies himself preparing the easel and palette, stepping opposite MONTY every time he has a message for him.*) I don't like painting generals. Still, what else can I do? I've got to live. (*To the* COLONEL, *turning away to get more equipment.*) He doesn't seem too sure about it, does he? (*Back in front of* MONTY.) One of the first casualties in war is art. I'll give you an example and a bloody tragic one. I've got a friend called Matthew Smith. I shouldn't think you've ever heard of him. But he's a damned good artist. Well he lost two sons in nineteen forty/ forty-one, and he hasn't put a brush to canvas since, poor bugger. And I can't say that I blame him. (*He starts to study him.*) Head round right. A bit more. Chin up. Right, now try and keep like that when we go into action.

MONTY: When will that be?

AUGUSTUS: When I've had a good look at you. You're in no hurry, are you?

MONTY: Generals are always in a hurry. That's right, isn't it, Joe?

COLONEL: Yes, sir.

AUGUSTUS: Blücher wasn't. Blücher dawdled.

MONTY: Blücher was an old man.

AUGUSTUS: You're no chicken, are you?

MONTY: Fifty-six.

AUGUSTUS: Then you're no chicken. Gott's death was your last chance, wasn't it?

MONTY: I couldn't say. I don't have your imagination.

AUGUSTUS: Well, I look at it like this. If his plane hadn't crashed, you'd still be fooling round Kent killing off your officers with early morning runs! (*To the COLONEL.*) Why hasn't he killed you yet?

COLONEL: Because I'm too healthy.

AUGUSTUS: Or you're too damned clever! I'll tell you what. You sprint away from HQ and the moment you're out of sight, you dive behind a haystack with a packet of fags.

MONTY: Joe says you're an OM.

AUGUSTUS: That's correct. You sound surprised.

MONTY: I am a bit, to judge from what I've seen here.

AUGUSTUS: That was my reaction when I got it.

MONTY: Why do you suppose you did?

DORELIA enters during the following.

AUGUSTUS: Because I'm a hard slogger. And the powers that be have got to stick their decorations somewhere. That's why your chest's like a public hoarding. And that's

34

why I only got the OM. Genii don't get them, they're too disruptive, only old hacks like us who go slogging on regardless of what damage we do. Yes – what is it, Dodo?

DORELIA: Will the general be staying to lunch?

MONTY: No, no – thank you. There's a scheme on that I've got to go and look at.

DORELIA starts to go.

AUGUSTUS: (*Stopping her going by addressing her.*) I've been telling him he drives his officers too hard. (*Pointing at the COLONEL.*) Except for this one who's too fly.

DORELIA: I've heard that, yes.

MONTY: Who have you heard it from?

DORELIA: Oh, little birds in pubs.

MONTY: In service dress and Sam Brownes?

DORELIA: Mostly, yes.

MONTY: What ranks?

DORELIA: All ranks.

MONTY: What pubs?

DORELIA: No names, no pack-drill, General.

AUGUSTUS: Well, we'd better get on, I suppose. Or we'll miss the Second Front. That's what you're being painted for, I take it. If it weren't, what's the hurry? When they rang me up, I said, "I'd rather do it in the summer, if I must." And they said, "You'll do it now, or never, maybe." And (*He points at DORELIA.*) she wouldn't let me turn it down. Because she said we'd starve!

DORELIA: He doesn't like to have to paint your kind of picture, General.

MONTY: I've gathered that.

DORELIA: He thinks it's unoriginal. But I say every portrait's unoriginal, because it has to have a model. But he says he much prefers to choose his own.

MONTY: And I don't blame him.

DORELIA: You're very understanding, General.

MONTY: I hope so.

DORELIA: Funny. People say exactly the reverse about you.

MONTY: Your friends in pubs!

DORELIA: Yes. They say you're overbearing – bigoted and humourless. They all say that without exception.

MONTY: When they're drunk.

DORELIA: *In vino veritas!*

AUGUSTUS: Don't worry, General. She says all those things about me. And not when she's drunk. But when I am! And they're not true either. Run along now, Dodo – I'm about to start on Bubbles.

The COLONEL turns away with a smile.

MONTY: Bubbles!

DORELIA: He invariably says that when he starts on a commercial portrait.

AUGUSTUS: You push off. And stop your chattering. (*He propels her to the door in a friendly manner, slapping her bottom.*)

DORELIA goes.

(*Returning to the easel and studying his model.*) She's getting old. She never used to speak when she was young. And now she can't stop chattering. I hope to God that, when she's in her dotage, she'll revert back. She was like an animal when she was young – and animals don't talk, thank God – a young deer in the evening sunlight – quavering and wide-eyed at the beauty of it all – the birch trees and the heather and the long dark shadows. Now she

36

finds the shadows overwhelming and depressing and the whole thing ugly – not excluding me – and so she shuts her eyes and chatters like a magpie instead. When's the Second Front?

MONTY: I don't know. And I wouldn't tell you if I did.

AUGUSTUS: You do know, General. But you're not saying.

MONTY: Then why ask me?

AUGUSTUS: Just to see if your eyes lit up.

MONTY: Did they?

AUGUSTUS: No – they flickered – that's all. And you can't catch flickers with a paintbrush, that's the bloody trouble. Have you ever heard of Buster Keaton?

MONTY: Yes, of course.

AUGUSTUS: Well, you're deadpan – like him. And I don't like painting deadpans.

COLONEL: You've done quite a lot of good ones, sir, if I may say so, in your time.

AUGUSTUS: Thank you for nothing.

COLONEL: It's a compliment, sir. It means you can do it even if you may not want to. That's the hallmark of a genius.

AUGUSTUS: Thank you for something – this time – young man. (*To MONTY.*) What's he doing in the Army?

MONTY: Looking after me.

AUGUSTUS: Why did you choose him – because he's good-looking?

MONTY: No, because he's got brains.

AUGUSTUS: What's that song? I know. "All the officers were playing leapfrog." (*He hums a little of it then sings again.*) "They were only playing leap-frog"…

MONTY: How do you know that?

AUGUSTUS: Because we used to sing it at the end of the last war.

MONTY: Where?

AUGUSTUS: In France.

MONTY: Why were you in France?

AUGUSTUS: Because I was a soldier of a sort.

MONTY: Oh! With what regiment?

AUGUSTUS: With the Canadians.

MONTY: Ah!

AUGUSTUS: What does "ah" mean?

MONTY: Take your choice. Belief – or disbelief. Or, merely, incredulity. What rank did you reach?

AUGUSTUS: Major.

MONTY: Ah!

AUGUSTUS: Don't keep saying "ah".

MONTY: Why shouldn't I? It's a free country. And it takes less breath to say "ah" than to say "Tell that to the Marines"!

AUGUSTUS: You don't believe it then.

MONTY: If you'd said "the Guards" I would have. They'll take anybody. Just as long as he can put his cap over his eyes and still keep marching on.

COLONEL: (*Who is one.*) He doesn't like the Guards, sir.

MONTY: Nonsense. I'm just pulling his leg.

AUGUSTUS: There are fairies at the bottom of my Guardsman!

MONTY: That's good. Very good, John. Where did you pick that up?

AUGUSTUS: In some pub or other.

MONTY: Very good. First class – Joe, don't let me forget it. And remind me to tell Alex. He'll like it. As he's got a sense of humour. Even if he hasn't got much else.

AUGUSTUS: I think the Guards are splendid.

COLONEL: They are splendid, sir. That's why he doesn't like them.

MONTY: Watch it, Joe – or you'll be posted back to them.

COLONEL: I just can't wait, sir.

MONTY: John – were you in uniform?

AUGUSTUS: Of course, I was – I was a major.

MONTY: So you had no beard then.

AUGUSTUS: Certainly I did.

MONTY: The Army don't allow beards. And they didn't then.

AUGUSTUS: Too bad! What about George the Fifth?

MONTY: He was the King.

AUGUSTUS: God bless him.

MONTY: Were you a war artist?

AUGUSTUS: Yes.

MONTY: I thought so. In the front line?

AUGUSTUS: Sometimes. Not too often though. I'm deaf you see, and so I couldn't hear the shells and I thought that was dangerous. Then the war stopped.

MONTY: And had you painted any pictures?

AUGUSTUS: Yes – the *Pageant of War.*

MONTY: Have I seen that, Joe?

COLONEL: I wouldn't know, sir.

MONTY: Have you?

COLONEL: Rather. And it's damned good.

AUGUSTUS: Sargent didn't think so.

MONTY: Sargent?

COLONEL: (*To MONTY.*) Sargent was a Yankee artist, sir.

AUGUSTUS: He thought that it was hideous.

MONTY: And was it?

AUGUSTUS: No more hideous than war.

MONTY: Where is it? I'd like to go and have a look at it.

AUGUSTUS: Don't ask me.

COLONEL: I'll find out for you, sir.

MONTY: Meanwhile – let's get on with the picture, shall we?

AUGUSTUS: Why not – that's what we're here for. (*To the COLONEL.*) You sit there behind me. And keep still (*He goes to his easel.*) Head round, left. More. Chin up. Right. Hold that. (*He starts to paint, or at least, sketch.*)

MONTY: Do you mind if I talk?

AUGUSTUS: I'd rather that you didn't. Do you mind if I don't?

MONTY: Please yourself.

AUGUSTUS: I don't like talking when I'm painting. I don't like my models talking either, as they can't keep still when they do. (*Jerking his hand back at the COLONEL.*) He can talk though, if he wants to.

COLONEL: What about, sir?

AUGUSTUS: Anything that takes your fancy. Women – choirboys – shoes, ships, cabbages or kings – whatever you think's going to be of interest to him.

COLONEL: (*To MONTY.*) What would you suggest, sir?

MONTY: That you keep your mouth shut!

COLONEL: That suits me, sir.

AUGUSTUS goes on painting MONTY with the COLONEL watching. Soon the COLONEL's head falls forward and he falls asleep. The Lights go down, time passes. The Lights come up again.

AUGUSTUS: *(At the easel, to MONTY.)* All right. You can get down now. *(To the COLONEL.)* And you can wake up.

COLONEL: Sorry, sir. I dropped off.

MONTY: So I noticed. *(To AUGUSTUS.)* May I have a look?

AUGUSTUS: No. It's a mess still.

MONTY: Why's that? Did you drink too much last night?

AUGUSTUS: No, sir, I don't think that you drank enough.

MONTY: I'd like to see it.

AUGUSTUS: Well, you can't. I'm in command here. *(He squints at the canvas again.)* You had no life in you. Not as much as a tin soldier. I'll have to get some interesting fellow in to talk to you tomorrow as you wouldn't let him.

MONTY: I know everything he's got to say, that's why. His mind's an open book to me. That's right, Joe, isn't it?

COLONEL: I wouldn't know, sir.

MONTY: I would.

COLONEL: Good for you, sir.

AUGUSTUS: I know – I'll get G.B.S. tomorrow. He can talk the hind leg off a donkey.

MONTY: That's what I'm afraid of. Not that I'm a donkey. I'm a soldier with a lot on his plate. And I like to think.

AUGUSTUS: You weren't thinking just now – you were like a dummy.

MONTY: I'll do better next time.

AUGUSTUS: I'm not risking it. I either pack it in or get Shaw.

MONTY: All right. Get Shaw. What's the time, Joe?

COLONEL: Twelve, sir.

MONTY: We're on parade at two. Well, I'll say good-morning, John.

AUGUSTUS: Good-morning, sir.

COLONEL: (*To AUGUSTUS.*) Good-morning, sir.

AUGUSTUS: Good-morning, Colonel. Don't forget, I'd like to paint you sometime.

MONTY: Better looking than me, is he?

AUGUSTUS: It was you that said it. (*To the COLONEL.*) Have you got a wife?

COLONEL: Yes, sir.

AUGUSTUS: Would she like you in uniform? Or p'raps she'd prefer a nude. I know I would if I was her.

COLONEL: I'll see if the car's there, sir.

The COLONEL goes.

MONTY: You embarrassed him.

AUGUSTUS: To find out what he's like.

MONTY: And what is he like?

AUGUSTUS: Sensitive. And shy. And frightened. And bewildered underneath that uniform. And beautiful.

MONTY: Are you a nancy-boy, John?

AUGUSTUS: No, regrettably. I've never had the time!

The COLONEL comes back.

COLONEL: The car's there, sir.

AUGUSTUS: (*To MONTY.*) See you tomorrow morning at eleven, if that suits you.

MONTY: I'll look forward to it.

AUGUSTUS: So will Shaw.

MONTY and the COLONEL go.

AUGUSTUS goes back to his easel and stands there looking at the canvas.

DORELIA comes in and busies herself clearing up things.

DORELIA: How did it go?

AUGUSTUS: It didn't.

DORELIA: Would you like some coffee?

AUGUSTUS: No thanks. I must work on it till lunch. He must have something after all those victories. I'm damned if I can see it though. Can you?

DORELIA: What? In him or the picture?

AUGUSTUS: Never mind the picture. In him.

DORELIA: Yes. His eyes. They're piercing.

AUGUSTUS: They're on that bloody canvas, are they?!

She goes round and stands beside him, looking at it.

DORELIA: *(Finally.)* No – not yet.

AUGUSTUS: They never will be – if he doesn't liven up. I'm getting Shaw to come round in the morning to amuse him.

DORELIA: I liked that young colonel.

AUGUSTUS: So did I. He's beautiful.

DORELIA: Did you tell Monty that?

AUGUSTUS: I did.

DORELIA: And what did he say?

AUGUSTUS: *(Imitating him.)* "John, are you a nancy-boy?" And I said "No, regrettably. Because I've never had the time." And then he pushed off.

DORELIA: I don't blame him.

AUGUSTUS: Dodo. Do you think he thought that I might make a pass at him?

DORELIA: I wouldn't be surprised.

AUGUSTUS: You're joking, Dodo.

DORELIA: Yes. Of course I am, you silly old goat.

AUGUSTUS: Go and ring up G.B.S. And ask him round tomorrow morning.

She turns to go out of the door.

That young colonel.

DORELIA: (*Stopping.*) Will be killed. I know, Gus.

AUGUSTUS: How do you know?

DORELIA: The same way as you do. Intuition. He reminded me of Pyramus. He would have been just like him if he'd lived.

AUGUSTUS: Well, thank God that he didn't.

DORELIA goes.

He stands there looking after her. He picks up his brush and attacks the canvas.

Blackout.

SCENE 2

The same. Twenty-four hours later.

The Lights come up on AUGUSTUS standing at his easel painting, MONTY keeps his pose, the young COLONEL sits where he was before, while G.B.S. sits upstage, between MONTY and AUGUSTUS.

A short silence.

G.B.S.: When you painted me, Augustus, if my memory serves me aright, you said I looked like an old goat. The phrase stuck in my memory because I was a young goat then, comparatively speaking.

AUGUSTUS: (*Holding his brush in a recriminatory way.*) G.B.S., I asked you here to talk to him (*Pointing the brush at MONTY.*) – not me. I'm busy. And he isn't. And the reason why I asked you is because he needs a clown to take his mind off what the Press calls "matters of great import".

G.B.S.: Clowns don't talk, Augustus. That's the beauty of them. They're like dogs with false noses. Everybody loves them. Whereas you and I talk far too much. That's why we make so many enemies. But we're still clowns.

AUGUSTUS: I'm not.

G.B.S.: No? Well, what else are you? Lurching round the streets of London, like a drunken, fornicating scarecrow, masquerading as a gypsy! Whereas I'm a pillar of respectability.

AUGUSTUS: Don't you believe him, General. He's nothing but a sanctimonious old hypocrite. And that's the last word that I'm going to say until this sitting's over. So it's over to you, G.B.S.

G.B.S.: It's not fair. It's like lobbing balls at an Aunt Sally.

AUGUSTUS: Talking balls more like. Still, that's what you're here for.

G.B.S.: All right, give me time. Just give me time. Don't rush me. I'm an old man. And my mind's a little sluggish in the morning. I can't jump straight in. I'm not an actor like you – splashing paint all over like confetti. I'm a thinking man and not a will-o'-the-wisp. I need planning and reconnaissance like he does.

MONTY looks round.

Don't you move, or you'll get me into trouble. Just absorb the compliment and make no comment. And then, if God's in His Heaven and Augustus has his paints mixed properly, he'll nail you for posterity. He nailed me once although it took a long, long time. (*To AUGUSTUS.*) Remember, Gus? (*Quickly.*) Forget it. (*He turns back to MONTY.*) When I've gone I've little doubt they'll stick it in the Garrick Club among the lesser lights of my profession. Not that Shakespeare's there because they never painted him. Or if they did, they couldn't get a taker, so they put a match to it to save the storage space!

AUGUSTUS: Don't listen to him, General. He's jealous, that's all. He knows he's a hack compared with Shakespeare.

G.B.S.: I thought you'd said your last word, Gus.

AUGUSTUS: I had until you started talking nonsense. Then I felt it necessary to interrupt you. Just in case my sitter thought that I agreed with you.

G.B.S.: Augustus is a fan of Shakespeare's, General, God knows why. Maybe, it's the bourgeois in him. Maybe, it's because he hasn't read him. Or sat through his dreary products like I've had to for the best part of my life. I used to be a drama critic – did you know that? Never mind, I'm telling you, if you were not aware of it. And that meant sitting through the whole lot, week in, week out, year in, year out, since they never stop presenting them. And did it get me down? Or didn't it? It sure did, as your Allies say. Of course there are some passages in Shakespeare that I'm ready to admit aren't all that bad. Antony's speech in the Forum for example, over Caesar's body. You'd need to be a bigot and a philistine of the first order to pronounce that that speech has no merit. It's chock full of merit. That's if you like melodrama – I don't personally all that much. It's good poetry, I grant you if you like that kind of poetry – which I don't. Anyway a theatre's no place for poetry unless you've gone in there deliberately to have a bit of shut-eye. It's for stimulation and excitement – not for recitation.

AUGUSTUS: Like my studio!

G.B.S.: What did you say, Gus?

AUGUSTUS: I said that my studio was not for recitation either.

G.B.S.: Well, what else can I do when you won't allow the man to talk.

AUGUSTUS: Shut up.

G.B.S.: I thought you asked me round to stop him looking like a stuffed owl.

AUGUSTUS: So I did. I didn't ask you round to bore his pants off, though.

G.B.S.: Field Marshal, am I boring you?

MONTY: John, leave to speak, sir?

AUGUSTUS: If you must.

MONTY: You're not, Shaw – funnily enough. Because I like to hear a rebel talking: I'm a bit of one myself.

G.B.S.: That's right. That's why I like you. You're my hero, General – or should I say Field Marshal. Did you know that?

AUGUSTUS: Don't you listen to him, General. He's talking Irish blarney. You're no more his hero than my arse is.

G.B.S.: Get on with your painting, Gus.

AUGUSTUS: I can't paint when I have to listen to a hypocritical old conshie oiling up to a field marshal. He's a conshie, General, and always has been. Ever since he hid behind his red beard in the nineteen fourteen war. If he lived anywhere but here, they'd shut him up for the duration and good riddance. But they don't. They let him blather on, destroying everyone's morale, including this young fellow's and then, if you please, as if that wasn't bad enough, he gets down on his knees and starts a sycophantic journey up your backside.

MONTY: Let's get on, John.

AUGUSTUS: When he's stopped his arse-crawling I will. Get back on Shakespeare, for God's sake before I fetch up, G.B.S.

G.B.S.: I was just going to – I was just about to say that you and Shakespeare had one thing in common.

AUGUSTUS: Genius.

G.B.S.: No, lack of humour. You can't tell when someone's joking, Gus. And I'd guess he couldn't either, judging by his inability to make a joke himself. You wouldn't know about his humour, General, or lack of it, if you've not been exposed to it all that much. So I'll tell you it's as heavy as your barrage was at Alamein and just about as lethal.

COLONEL: You really mean all that, sir, do you? Or are you just pulling our legs?

G.B.S.: What do you think?

COLONEL: I'm not sure, sir.

G.B.S.: Well, I'll tell you. Life's a leg-pull. If it wasn't, there'd be no sense in it. We'd all go mad. Not just occasionally, like now – but permanently. You can thank your stars, young man, that you're only dressed like that for the duration. When your boss has driven back the infidel with fire and sword and Churchill tanks, you can come home and dress like me or (*Pointing at AUGUSTUS*.) him, according to your preference and sink back thankfully into your normal abnormality; by which I mean the normal lunacies the human race indulges in from day to day – the crossword puzzle in whatever paper takes your fancy, the eternal struggle with the bind-weed in your garden, the lifelong and comforting preoccupation with the working of your bowels. Indeed, you wouldn't ask me such a question as you asked just now in peace-time. You'd be content to let me wallow in my studied eccentricity. But now that you're balanced on the very edge of reason, you're desperate to stamp out any sign of nonconformity – for fear it should unbalance your pathetically inadequate facade of equilibrium. You dress up in that spotless suit of clothes from Huntsman in the hope that it may help you to retain the last remaining shred of sanity at the disposal of your tortured little soul.

The COLONEL looks tortured.

MONTY: I'm sorry but I can't take any more of this, John.

AUGUSTUS: I don't blame you. Shut up, G.B.S.

G.B.S.: Why should I? Aren't I here to stir him up? (*Turning back to MONTY.*) You can't take any more of it because you've got that double-breasted beret on, which means that you're trying to preserve a touch of individuality instead of settling for an automaton. And that won't do in wartime, if you want to insulate yourself against its bestiality and agony like he does.

AUGUSTUS: Leave him out of it, for God's sake.

G.B.S.: All right I'll concentrate on you, Field Marshal, since Augustus thinks the Colonel's too young for this sort of conversation. What I find intriguing about you is that a soldier of your calibre and ingenuity should feel it necessary to be an exhibitionist as well. But I know why you do it. It's because you're quite a modest little fellow and of the opinion that you lack charisma which is an opinion, since we're on the subject that I wouldn't for one minute quarrel with! In consequence, in order to compete with Rommel's buccaneering spirit and his goggles and his high-peaked cap, you stick your RAC badge on your beret next to your AA badge or whatever and you hit him for six out of Africa. And that's why you're my hero, General. Because, apart from all the squalor and the sorrow and the sacrifice, you've won the admiration of an army and a nation and its allies with a single safety-pin! Have you a drink, Augustus, in this house that isn't alcoholic?

AUGUSTUS: Anything to stop you talking! Coffee – water. Which would you prefer?

G.B.S.: I wouldn't say no to a glass of water.

AUGUSTUS: General?

MONTY: No thank you.

AUGUSTUS: Colonel?

COLONEL: No, sir, thank you.

AUGUSTUS: You can get up, General, and stretch your legs. But not in the direction of my easel. (*Opening the door and calling.*) Dodo, could you bring a glass of water. The glass in here's full of paint. I'm sorry, but my mind's on my work. (*He turns back and then has an afterthought.*) And a glass of wine for me!

DORELIA: (*Off.*) There isn't any.

AUGUSTUS: Then nip out and buy a bottle.

MONTY: (*To the COLONEL.*) What's it like?

AUGUSTUS: Don't tell him.

MONTY: It's an order!

AUGUSTUS: Disobey it, Colonel!

> *The COLONEL looks from MONTY to AUGUSTUS.*

Disobey it. Or I'll chuck it on the floor and stamp on it.

COLONEL: (*To MONTY.*) It's interesting, sir.

MONTY: I should hope so. I'm an interesting man.

COLONEL: (*Dutifully.*) That's right, sir.

G.B.S.: (*Rising.*) Do you really think that, Colonel – or are you just saying it to please him?

MONTY: Naturally, he's saying it because it's what he believes – and quite rightly.

G.B.S.: Is it, Colonel? Do you really think he's interesting? Or do you merely stand in awe of him like any schoolboy with a dormitory monitor who's handy with a slipper?

MONTY: He admires me. Don't you Joe? Immensely.

G.B.S.: Let him answer for himself.

AUGUSTUS: Unless he feels he's got to lie. (*To the COLONEL.*) In which case, I suggest you keep quiet.

COLONEL: There's no need to answer, sir – because the answer's obvious.

AUGUSTUS: Well said, young man. You've got your head screwed on the right way.

MONTY: That's why I employ him!

AUGUSTUS: He's got everything screwed on the right way has our drummer boy, if you ask me. That's why I want to paint him. Did you ask your wife how she'd like you done?

COLONEL: In uniform, sir.

AUGUSTUS: What a disappointment! I was looking forward to a naked figure standing by a lake. And looking down at its reflection in the water with thanksgiving for the gifts of youth and beauty and virility. Still, if she wants you to herself – and I can't say I blame her – then I'll do it in a uniform for free. When can I start?

COLONEL: On my next leave, sir.

AUGUSTUS: When's that?

COLONEL: In six months' time, sir. I've just had my last one.

AUGUSTUS: I'll look forward to it.

MONTY: You'll have finished mine by then, I hope.

AUGUSTUS: I hope so too.

MONTY: You're not enjoying it then?

AUGUSTUS: What? The painting, period? Or painting you?

MONTY: The latter.

AUGUSTUS: Since you ask the only thing I like about it is the money. It's not your fault. To tell you the truth, I don't like painting anybody much, not since this bloody war began. Well, maybe one in ten but not more. What I want's a bigger canvas if I'm going to go on painting. You got bored with square-bashing I would imagine, when you realized that there were bigger things ahead of you in your profession. Well there's bigger things in mine.

MONTY: What things?

AUGUSTUS: What things? Just listen to him! Go and squint up at the ceiling in the Sistine Chapel sometime, if you get through this war, and you'll soon find out. It's things like that an artist should be working on these days, not on bloody little postage stamps like this. (*He makes a gesture at the canvas.*) Apart from that, you're not the kind of subject that appeals to me. I'd rather paint a gypsy or a tart and, through no fault of your own, you're neither. Or a mistress, past or present – or to come. And you don't qualify in that field either. You're a soldier, in a uniform with something on his mind. And I don't like it. That's why I can't stick it on the bloody canvas. But don't worry – I'll keep trying as I need the money. (*Pointing at the COLONEL.*) But I'd still much rather paint him, and, I'll tell you why – because he's different. And I'll tell you why he's different. Because he's got something on his mind that I can understand. Because it's something that's on mine as well. And I'll tell you what it is. He hates this bloody war like hell. And you don't – you enjoy it. I'm not blaming you because it's your job – don't misunderstand me. If you didn't like it, you'd be a mountebank and a disgrace to your profession. All I'm saying is that I don't want to paint a predator. I'd rather paint its victim while it's still in one piece, even though it'd break my heart.

DORELIA comes in with a glass of water, an open bottle of wine and an empty glass.

MONTY: Good-morning.

DORELIA: Morning, General. Good-morning, Colonel. (*She turns to G.B.S.*) Morning, G.B.S.

G.B.S.: Good-morning, Dodo. (*Taking the water.*) Would it be in order if I said you look a picture?

DORELIA: An old master, like you?

G.B.S.: An immortal.

DORELIA: Thank you. Shall I pour your wine, Gus?

AUGUSTUS: If you don't mind washing up the glass.

DORELIA: (*Pouring the wine.*) I hope you've done your duty, G.B.S.

AUGUSTUS: Has he not!

DORELIA: Well beyond the call of – sometimes I expect. Would that be correct, General?

MONTY: Yes. Absolutely spot on.

G.B.S.: You're implying that I shocked you, are you?

MONTY: If you like, Shaw, yes.

G.B.S.: But I was play-acting. I don't normally talk like that. I'm a retiring, modest, sober citizen by nature. But my orders were to try and stimulate your mind. I'm sure whatever he may say, in his perversity, Augustus caught a look in your eye in this morning's session that he couldn't catch with his brush yesterday.

AUGUSTUS: (*With his glass of wine.*) That's right.

G.B.S.: You see!

AUGUSTUS: And how I wish to God I hadn't.

DORELIA: What does that mean?

AUGUSTUS: What it says. And what I've just been saying!

MONTY: (*After a pause.*) I'd like to see it, John.

AUGUSTUS: Well, you can't.

MONTY: Why not? I'm entitled to. It's me you're painting, isn't it? I don't see why I've got to sit here like some tailor's dummy, without knowing what you're up to. If you're too ashamed to show it to me, I suggest we call the whole thing off.

AUGUSTUS: That suits me.

DORELIA: No it doesn't, Gus. We need the money.

MONTY: Well said, madam.

AUGUSTUS: (*To MONTY.*) All right, please yourself. But don't blame me, if you don't like it.

MONTY moves round and stands looking at it. DORELIA stays, watching.

MONTY: What's the idea of that blue cloud over my head?

AUGUSTUS: Don't ask me.

MONTY: I'm asking you. I don't go round with blue clouds floating round my head, John – do I?

AUGUSTUS: Not so you'd notice.

MONTY: Well, why put it in?

AUGUSTUS: Why not? I felt like putting it in.

MONTY: That's not good enough.

AUGUSTUS: It's good enough for me.

MONTY: It's not the sort of picture that I'd like to leave my son.

AUGUSTUS: Too bad.

MONTY: I don't want it, in fact. Not unless it's going to get a great deal better. (*To DORELIA.*) Is it?

DORELIA: We'll have to wait and see.

MONTY: How long?

DORELIA: Until he's worked on it.

MONTY: I see. (*Turning back to AUGUSTUS.*) You want to go on now?

AUGUSTUS: I've no alternative. Not with that money-grabbing harridan's eye on me!

DORELIA goes, winking at MONTY as she does so.

MONTY resumes his pose. Augustus starts painting.

MONTY: (*After a while.*) Don't forget to paint out that blue cloud.

AUGUSTUS: (*Stopping painting.*) Don't tell me what to do, or I'll pack it in!

MONTY: Well, think about it – that's all I ask – think about it.

AUGUSTUS: I'll think about it, if you'll do something for me.

MONTY: What's that?

AUGUSTUS: Stop chattering!

MONTY looks dumbfounded and is rendered speechless.

And G.B.S.

G.B.S.: Yes?

AUGUSTUS: You start chattering again.

G.B.S.: The trouble is I've lost my continuity of thought.

AUGUSTUS: It's news to me you ever had it!

G.B.S.: You're not meant to listen, Gus. You're meant to concentrate on painting the field marshal for posterity.

MONTY: Shaw. I'm not a field marshal.

G.B.S.: Never mind. You will be soon. (*To the COLONEL.*) What was I talking about when I called for a drink, young man?

COLONEL: Safety-pins, sir.

G.B.S.: That's right. I was saying that you are my hero, General. And the world's pin-up.

MONTY: You'd better not tell Ike that.

AUGUSTUS: Keep still.

MONTY: Sorry.

AUGUSTUS: : Chin up. Not so much. Right. And keep quiet in future or I'll pack it in.

Silence again.

G.B.S.: You don't get on with Ike, of course. Because you're just the kind of Englishman Americans can't stand. And I don't blame them.

MONTY: (*To AUGUSTUS.*) Leave to speak, sir.

AUGUSTUS: If you don't move.

MONTY: I'm an Irishman, Shaw.

G.B.S.: You're an Ulsterman. And that's worse than two Englishmen to an American. And to a pure-bred Irishman like me, it's worse than three. Since Gus said I was a hypocritical old conshie earlier, Field Marshal, I've been wondering if you've been wondering what he is. Well, I'll tell you.

AUGUSTUS: Careful, G.B.S. Or I'll stop working again.

G.B.S.: Then your sitter won't think very much of you, if you ask me, because he's fighting for my right to answer back. And I'd be ungrateful if I didn't take advantage of it. Just as you'd be a Fascist if you didn't let me. (*Having effectively argued AUGUSTUS out of it, he turns to MONTY.*) When he went to France in the first war, Field Marshal, in his uniform and splashed a lot of paint around he thought that he was Foch and Haig rolled into one. And he's not over it yet. But he wasn't. And he isn't. He's got the same views as I have underneath his truculence. But, unlike me, he hasn't got the guts to say so in the presence of the top-brass.

AUGUSTUS: Watch it!

G.B.S.: What he should be doing is attempting to persuade you to nip round to see old Winston and say. "Listen, you old warhorse. Leave the prosecution of the war to me and get on with the peace-making."

AUGUSTUS: Ignore him, sir. He's talking nonsense.

G.B.S.: Am I? I just wonder. And I also wonder if the general's not wondering too. Soldiers aren't like you were, Gus, in the last war. They're pros. They're face to face with life. And death. And nothing concentrates the mind so wonderfully as that. I wouldn't be at all surprised if the field marshal wouldn't like to see old Winston playing politics again, by offering the boys in Germany who don't like Hitler peace-terms so that they can knock him off his perch on their own. Otherwise you'll have to do it for them when you've caught the Nazis with their trousers down. And that'll pose a problem for you. And I wouldn't like to have to solve it. Not that the decision will be yours or even Eisenhower's. It'll be Winston's, Roosevelt's and Stalin's. And if you can name three more unprincipled old rascals to have ever sat together in an apple cart I'll take my hat off to you. They'll be sanctimonious of course, and no-one more so than that sanctimonious old Groucho Marx from Georgia. And Roosevelt and Winston'll be sentimental. And I don't know which is worse. And I'll bet my bottom dollar there'll be a compromise. And that'll mean a trial, which for sheer hypocrisy'll rival anything that Pontius Pilate ever washed his hands of!

AUGUSTUS: Why should it be hypocritical to try your enemies for war crimes?

G.B.S.: Because we've committed the same crimes ourselves.

AUGUSTUS: What? Rounding up the Jews for God's sake!

G.B.S.: No, not that one, thank the Lord. But all the others. Bombing non-military targets for one.

AUGUSTUS: We had no choice, G.B.S. We're fighting for democracy and freedom, aren't we? Whereas, they're fighting for dictatorship and Nazism.

G.B.S.: They've got no choice either.

AUGUSTUS: Balls.

G.B.S.: It's not balls. Not unless the military code is balls.

AUGUSTUS: And I'll bet you think it is!

G.B.S.: That's not the point. It's what they think that matters. And they've sworn an oath of loyalty like he has. And, in consequence, they're obliged to honour it, regardless of what figure-head they swore it at, whether the king or Hitler. And you propose to punish them for doing that – not only on the battlefield but in a court of law so called, when it's all over. Well if that isn't hypocrisy, I'd like to know what is.

AUGUSTUS: It's talking like you when you're sitting pretty in a democratic country and you know damned well you wouldn't be allowed to under Hitler.

G.B.S.: That's exactly my point. But you're far too thick to see it!

AUGUSTUS turns away, throwing down his brush.

MONTY: (*After a pause.*) Shaw.

G.B.S.: Sir.

MONTY: You're interfering with the sitting.

G.B.S.: Sorry. But Gus got my goat.

MONTY: No more than you got his. So I suggest you shake hands on it.

G.B.S.: Hearken to the peacemaker! All right, Gus.

They shake.

But you'll feel like I do, one day, mark my words, when you're as mature as I am. (*Wagging his finger at him.*) Think of me when you do. All right, carry on. And I'll go and talk to this young man as the field marshal seems to find me irritating. (*He sits near the COLONEL.*)

MONTY: Mischievous that's all, Shaw. And subversive. And don't try it on him, or I'll get him to arrest you.

AUGUSTUS picks up his brush again.

AUGUSTUS: Chin up just a little.

G.B.S.: Well, what shall we talk about, young man?

AUGUSTUS: Left a shade.

COLONEL: Whatever you like, sir.

AUGUSTUS: Right. Hold it.

G.B.S.: Have you seen any of my plays?

COLONEL: Yes, quite a few, sir.

G.B.S.: And which one's your favourite?

MONTY: He's not said that he likes any of them, yet, Shaw.

AUGUSTUS: Sit still.

G.B.S.: And keep quiet, Field Marshal. If I've given up my conversation with you in your interest, you should give up yours with me in mine! (*To the COLONEL.*) Which one did you like best?

COLONEL: *St Joan*, sir.

G.B.S.: You've got good taste. Sybil Thorndike, was it?

COLONEL: Yes I think so. I was very young.

G.B.S.: How did you find her?

COLONEL: Who, sir? Sybil Thorndike or St Joan?

G.B.S. Joan. Sybil was inspired. But did you think that Joan was too? Or just a crackpot?

COLONEL: Oh, inspired, sir.

G.B.S.: By God? Or ambition?

COLONEL: God, I would have thought, sir.

G.B.S.: You're a believer then?

COLONEL: Oh yes, sir.

G.B.S.: I'm not.

COLONEL: So I've heard, sir.

G.B.S.: Do you think I'll go to Hell?

COLONEL: I wouldn't know, sir.

G.B.S.: God's a funny fellow, isn't He? You never know what He'll be up to next. One day He'll come up trumps as far as His admirers are concerned. The next He'll kick them in the teeth. But does that put them off Him? Not at all. They come up for more. Do you go to church? I don't mean in the army, where you've got to. But at home?

COLONEL: Oh, yes, sir.

G.B.S.: When you want something?

COLONEL: Or when I've got something, sir. Like my baby daughter.

G.B.S.: Who you're in love with obviously.

COLONEL: Yes, sir – and my wife.

G.B.S.: So God's on your side at the moment?

COLONEL: Yes, sir.

G.B.S.: Long may He remain there.

AUGUSTUS looks round.

COLONEL: Thank you, sir.

G.B.S.: I used to talk to Charlotte – my wife –

The COLONEL nods.

about God a lot. Or, to be more precise, she used to talk to me a lot about Him. And there wasn't any stopping her. She seemed to think that He'd be waiting for her when she turned her toes up like the door-keeper at *Claridge's* or the *Savoy*. Of course, I always told her, it's a lot of mumbo-jumbo, that there's no one waiting for her but a fellow with a can of petrol and a matchbox. But she just smiled at me and said "Oh indeed there is" with that daft look of confidence in her eye that I'd not seen since an uncle took me to the Curragh when I was a lad. My mother's brother it was. And he hadn't picked a winner since the Battle of the Boyne! "Indeed there is", she used to say. And when I stood there in the crematorium I thought to myself, "Charlotte, old friend, that's a funny way to go and meet your maker, skidding down a runway like a suitcase on the ramp at Northolt Airport and it isn't only faith that'll be wanted, I thought to myself, if you're going to meet Him face to face. He's going to need one hell of an imagination, like your own." When I die – and I've got an idea that it won't be very long now – I'll not be hoping for the kind of immortality that Charlotte wanted. I'll be quite happy with the immortality that I've already earned with my dramatic genius. Which other of my plays did you like?

He gets no answer and looks across at the COLONEL *and finds that he has nodded off.*

Gus, the Colonel's asleep.

AUGUSTUS: Can you blame him?

G.B.S.: I suppose not. In fact, I think it's a good wheeze. Good-night, Gus. Good-night, Field Marshal. (*He closes his eyes.*)

AUGUSTUS paints on. The Lights fade again – to denote the passage of time. The Lights come up again. They sleep on.

DORELIA comes in.

DORELIA: Gus, the driver's here.

The COLONEL *and* G.B.S. *wake on her entry.*

AUGUSTUS: Thank God. All right, you can wake up now, G.B.S.

MONTY: Are you not going on? I'm in no hurry.

AUGUSTUS: Not this morning. I don't feel like it. Not that I ever did. But I feel like it even less than usual at the moment. All right, General, you can get down now.

MONTY: (*Getting down.*) Have you painted out that blue cloud?

AUGUSTUS: No. I've added to it. It's red, white and blue now!

MONTY: You're joking!

AUGUSTUS: As you say I'm joking.

MONTY: So it's scrapped?

AUGUSTUS: You'll find out when it's finished, won't you?

MONTY: Fair enough. Well, thank you, John. (*He holds out his hand.*) You're an artist and you need to go your own way.

AUGUSTUS: (*Shaking hands.*) That's right.

MONTY: Better luck in future.

AUGUSTUS: (*Impressed.*) Thank you.

G.B.S.: (*Getting up.*) Can I cadge a lift from you, Field Marshal?

MONTY: Certainly – where do you want to go to?

G.B.S.: Hertfordshire. Ayot St Lawrence.

MONTY: All right. When he's dropped us at the War Office my driver'll deliver you there.

G.B.S.: Thank you. Will he want a tip?

MONTY: Don't ask me. Ask him.

G.B.S.: It's an order, is it?

MONTY: Don't ask me. Ask him. (*He turns to AUGUSTUS.*) Well goodbye, John. When's our next session?

G.B.S. sits again.

AUGUSTUS: When I've spent some time on it, I'll ring you.

MONTY: When will that be?

AUGUSTUS: In the morning, maybe. Maybe, the next morning. Maybe next week. Maybe sometime. Maybe never.

DORELIA: Pay no attention to him, General. He's just being difficult. He'll get it right.

MONTY: I hope so. Goodbye, madam. I've enjoyed meeting you. Ready, Shaw?

G.B.S.: If I can get up. Yes, I'm ready. Goodbye, Gussie. You'll manage as you're a genius. And genii can do the most unlikely things, as we both know. (*He looks at the picture.*) It's not bad. Not at all bad. But don't paint it over like you did with mine. The field marshal won't like it. Goodbye, Dodo. Thanks for the refreshment.

DORELIA: I'll see you all down.

COLONEL: Sorry that I fell asleep, sir.

G.B.S.: It was your loss, not mine, young man.

DORELIA ushers out MONTY and G.B.S..

The COLONEL is about to follow them.

AUGUSTUS: You've not said goodbye to me, young man.

COLONEL: Goodbye, sir. It's been thrilling meeting you.

AUGUSTUS: Well, come and shake hands.

The COLONEL goes towards him and AUGUSTUS takes his hand.

COLONEL: Sorry that I fell asleep, sir.

AUGUSTUS: I don't blame you. I invariably do the same when I go to his plays.

COLONEL: I'm sure you don't. You're joking.

AUGUSTUS: Maybe.

COLONEL: I'm afraid I missed a lot. But I was dead-tired as I couldn't sleep last night.

AUGUSTUS: Why? What was on your mind.

COLONEL: Oh, I don't know. (*He lowers his head shyly, and then looks up again.*) I kept on worrying about my wife and daughter if I get killed.

AUGUSTUS: (*Not too convincingly.*) You won't get killed.

COLONEL: If I don't, I'm going to be an artist like you.

AUGUSTUS: Good luck to you.

COLONEL: Thank you, sir.

AUGUSTUS: (*Finding it hard to control his emotions.*) You'd better run along now or you'll get a bollocking from the field marshal.

COLONEL: (*Turning to go.*) I'll ring you when I come on leave, sir.

AUGUSTUS: (*Gruffly, his voice breaking.*) Do that, Colonel, do that.

The COLONEL, understanding AUGUSTUS's emotion, turns round and goes out, putting on his cap.

Augustus picks up the wine bottle, drinks a long draught, puts it down and stares.

DORELIA comes back.

DORELIA: You're being very silly, Gus. If you're not careful you'll lose your money.

AUGUSTUS: I'll sell it for much more to someone else, so don't you worry.

DORELIA starts a bit of tidying. He goes on staring ahead.

DORELIA: (*Going over to him.*) What's the matter, Gus?

AUGUSTUS: I can't paint any more – not like I used to.

DORELIA: Yes, of course you can.

AUGUSTUS: I can't.

DORELIA: You can. Or, rather, you could if you knocked off this. (*She picks up the bottle of wine.*)

AUGUSTUS: Give me that bottle.

DORELIA: But you're working.

AUGUSTUS: (*Roaring at her.*) Give me back that bottle.

She puts it down on the table.

I'm not working any more today. I've better things to do. (*He takes a long swig.*)

She goes to the door with the glass G.B.S. drank from, looks back, then puts it down and comes back.

DORELIA: Gus, I can sympathize.

AUGUSTUS: Why don't you then?

DORELIA: Because I want to give you strength.

AUGUSTUS: What for?

DORELIA: To go on working.

AUGUSTUS: I told Monty about Matthew packing it in just now. And I said I didn't blame him. I know just how he felt, Dodo.

DORELIA: No, you don't. Don't make a martyr of yourself. You've been much luckier than him. You've not lost anybody yet. So thank your stars for that. (*She goes to the door and then turns back.*) I'll tell you what I'm going to do, Gus, now I come to think of it. It'll do you good and might just stop you thinking only of yourself.

AUGUSTUS: What's that?

DORELIA: Ask Matthew to stay in the country sometime.

AUGUSTUS: What the devil for?

DORELIA: Well, you could try and get him painting again. It'd do you good and might do him good, too.

AUGUSTUS: The blind leading the blind.

DORELIA: If you're blind you know why, Gus. (*She turns and goes towards the door.*)

AUGUSTUS: That boy won't be coming back on leave.

DORELIA: (*Stopping by the door.*) I know. I know that just as well as you do.

AUGUSTUS looks very sad.

But life must go on.

AUGUSTUS: I wish to God it didn't have to.

DORELIA: Yes, I know you do. But you'll feel better when you've had a sleep, and, then, you'll finish Monty's picture.

AUGUSTUS: I don't want to finish it.

DORELIA: I know you don't just now. But you will, Gus.

AUGUSTUS: I won't.

DORELIA: You will. Because you're a genius, as G.B.S. just said.

This does not comfort him.

You're blaming Monty for the death of that young man.

AUGUSTUS: That's right, I am.

DORELIA: Well, don't – because it isn't his fault. Any more than it's your fault or mine.

AUGUSTUS: Whose is it then?

DORELIA: You'd better ask God that. Or G.B.S.!

She smiles her quiet smile, picks the glass up and goes.

He drains the bottle, picks his brush up and attacks the canvas, and then leans forward with his forehead resting on it and his shoulders heaving.

Fade to Blackout.

SCENE 3

Fryern Court, Hampshire. October, 1944

The Lights come up on AUGUSTUS standing behind his easel painting MATTHEW SMITH, a quiet, bald man wearing thick spectacles.

AUGUSTUS: (*Pausing to contemplate his work.*) I'll tell you something, Matthew. This one's going to be damned good.

No reply.

You heard what I said, did you?

MATTHEW: Yes.

AUGUSTUS: I'm sorry. But it's difficult to tell – you're so damned quiet. One doesn't know if you're registering or not. If you're not careful I'll send for G.B.S. How would you like that?

MATTHEW: Not at all. (*After a pause.*) I'm a quiet man. So I suggest you paint a quiet man.

AUGUSTUS: That's exactly what I'm doing.

MATTHEW: And you think it's going to be good?

AUGUSTUS: Bloody good.

MATTHEW: Then carry on.

AUGUSTUS starts again.

AUGUSTUS: (*After a silence.*) I've not done much of this, have you?

MATTHEW: What?

AUGUSTUS: Painting fellow daubers.

MATTHEW: No.

AUGUSTUS: I've painted myself often. But then I'm a damned good model. Fiery and flamboyant. And more often pissed than not. All the correct things. Whereas you're like old Dodgson's dormouse looking longingly towards the teapot with a view to tucking up inside it. Still, I'm quite enjoying myself.

MATTHEW: Good.

AUGUSTUS: And when I've finished, you're going to start on me.

MATTHEW: No, Gus.

AUGUSTUS: You are. That's the whole idea. Dodo's planned it that way. That's why you've been asked to stay. You mustn't think we asked you to the country for ten days just for the pleasure of your company. There's a design behind the whole thing. It's a wicked plot. And I've just given it away to you. But someone had to. Sometime. You've been here five days already and there's not much time left.

MATTHEW: Sorry. But I'm never going to paint again.

AUGUSTUS: Not ever?

MATTHEW: Never.

AUGUSTUS: (*After a pause.*) How long is it since you packed it in?

MATTHEW: Three years.

AUGUSTUS: What are you going to do instead?

MATTHEW: Die, I hope.

AUGUSTUS: Die. Come off it, Matthew. You're talking nonsense. You're younger than me. You've got years of painting in you yet. A damned sight more than I have, if you ask me. (*He paints on, then stops again.*) Do you know I very nearly did the same as you this August.

MATTHEW: Did what?

AUGUSTUS: Chucked the towel in. And for the same reason. Very nearly, anyway. (*He puts down his palette.*) Let's knock off for a while, I'm talking too much. And I'll bugger up my little masterpiece if I don't watch it. (*He pours out a glass of wine.*) Like to join me?

MATTHEW: No, thanks.

AUGUSTUS: (*Sitting down on a stool near MATTHEW.*) It was Mark and Dermot getting killed that finished you off, wasn't it? No need to answer. It goes without saying. France, in nineteen forty, didn't do you any good at all. And nor did losing half your pictures. But when both your sons went, one after the other, it was too much for you. So you packed it in. And I'm not blaming you. I'd do the same if Caspar went, most likely. Although how long it'd last I wouldn't like to say, because, unlike you, I'm a selfish bugger, not cut out for martyrdom in any way. But as I say, I damned near threw the towel in back in August when I read one morning in *The Times* that a young colonel in the Guards had been killed outside Caen. He wasn't a relation. He was just a staff officer who came to Tite Street when I painted Monty in the spring before the Second Front. But he was everything that makes life worthwhile all rolled into one. Good-looking, sensitive, attractive, decent. Innocent and lovable. And I knew he was going to die. And so did Dodo. And when I read his name in that list, I saw for the first time, the full enormity of war. It's total, undiluted bestiality. It hit me like a bloody sledgehammer between the eyes. (*He slaps his forehead.*) Just like that but a damned sight harder. I'd never liked it, mark you, much. But I'd tolerated it and thought it was a necessary evil up to then. And I suppose that I'd admired the trappings and the glamour of it. But, when it claimed that enchanting boy who hoped to be an artist at the end of it, if he survived, I knew one couldn't make excuses for it any more. It wasn't to be tolerated for another second – necessary evil or preventive medicine, whatever anybody cared to call it. It was out for the duration and to be denounced on every suitable occasion. That's what happened to me, Matthew, when I read about that boy's death. And I'm not surprised it happened to you under infinitely worse conditions. It's the penalty, I should imagine, that we artists pay for being what we are. I guess the ordinary fellow isn't faced with the same problem. But the likes of you and me who live on our imaginations, either pack it in, like you did, and decide the world's too bloody awful for one to continue making any contributions to its welfare. Or like me, decide to compromise and go on painting in the same way as a CO goes minesweeping to preserve his raison d'être in a world that he disapproves of and, indeed, abhors. And, so far it's worked, Matthew, though I'm not pretending that I think that that makeshift solution's going to last me for a lifetime. But it's working now. And I'd like to think that it'd work with you, too, if you were prepared to let it. (*He looks at him.*) Which, I take it, you're not.

MATTHEW: That's right. I'm sorry, Gus, but that's right.

AUGUSTUS: Don't be sorry. But, nonetheless, I can't help thinking it's a pity. Just as it'd be a pity if the sun decided not to come out any more. (*He gets up off his stool.*) Well, I'd better get back to my dormouse. (*He puts down his glass and goes back to his easel, picks up his palette. Then he has an idea and goes to the door. Calling.*) Dodo.

DORELIA: (*Off.*) Yes, Gus.

AUGUSTUS: (*Calling.*) Come in here and talk to Matthew. What're you doing?

DORELIA: (*Off.*) Crocheting.

AUGUSTUS: (*Calling.*) Well, come and do it in here. (*He turns back, leaving the door open. To MATTHEW.*) Have you ever tried it?

MATTHEW: No.

AUGUSTUS: I have. And made a dreadful balls-up of it.

DORELIA comes in.

Come and talk to Matthew. I can't make him see sense.

DORELIA: What about – his painting?

AUGUSTUS: Yes.

DORELIA: (*Looking at the canvas as she passes it.*) That's very good, Gus.

AUGUSTUS: Glad you like it – I do too. And I hope Matthew's going to as well.

DORELIA: I'm quite sure he will. (*She sits down.*) So much so, in fact, that he'll feel duty bound to paint you back.

AUGUSTUS: He says he won't. He'd rather die than paint, he says – the silly old sod.

DORELIA: He's younger than you, Gus.

AUGUSTUS: I daresay. But he's cracked sooner, that's all. (*To MATTHEW.*) I'm not saying that you hadn't every known excuse for doing so. I'm merely saying you did for the record. (*To DORELIA.*) I was telling him, if I'd lost Caspar or one of the others, let alone two, I'd have done the same.

But I've been spared that so far, thank the Lord, although what's going to happen in this bloody war before it finishes God knows, unless, of course, He's got himself pissed like a wise man, and passed out for the duration.

DORELIA: Matthew, can I ask you something?

MATTHEW nods.

What do you think Mark and Dermot would have thought about you giving up your painting?

MATTHEW: I can't tell you.

DORELIA: I can tell you. They would both have heartily deplored it.

MATTHEW: That's just a guess.

DORELIA: And a pretty good one if you ask me. They admired you, Matthew, passionately. Just like Gus and I do.

MATTHEW: Oh, yes!

DORELIA: (*Repeating it.*) Oh, yes, Matthew.

He still looks dubious.

Do you know what Gus said to me once?

MATTHEW: About me?

DORELIA: Yes.

MATTHEW: I'd rather not know.

DORELIA: Wait until you've heard it. We were at an exhibition of yours, standing looking at one of your nudes. And Gus pointed at your name across the canvas and said, "That's a funny way of spelling Rubens".

MATTHEW: Did you say that, Gus?

AUGUSTUS: I daresay. If it was a private view and I'd had a swig or two of champagne on an empty stomach!

DORELIA: You did say it, Gus. What's more, you meant it, didn't you?

AUGUSTUS: Yes, if you say so.

DORELIA: He's just being cagey, Matthew. Like a small boy who's not going to tell his best friend he believes in God in case he sneaks.

AUGUSTUS goes on painting with a faint smile.

(*Trying again.*) I lost my first child, Matthew. Pyramus. He died when he was eight of meningitis.

MATTHEW: I remember, Dodo.

DORELIA: But I didn't give up.

MATTHEW: You're a woman. Women are invincible.

DORELIA: Gus didn't either. He just went on working.

MATTHEW: He explained why just now. He said he was selfish.

DORELIA: You're the one who's being selfish, Matthew, now.

MATTHEW: Me?

DORELIA: Yes. By robbing everyone of future masterpieces – not to speak of lessening the fame of Mark and Dermot's family and thus diminishing their share of immortality.

MATTHEW registers this strongly.

AUGUSTUS: I've finished. (*He puts down his palette and picks up his glass.*) You can have a squint now, Matthew, if you want to.

MATTHEW gets up and goes round the canvas and stands looking at it without a word.

Well, what do you think?

MATTHEW: It's marvellous, Gus. Thank you.

MATTHEW holds out his hand. AUGUSTUS shakes it, then takes the canvas off the easel and puts it down against the wall, replacing it with a bare canvas.

Don't tell me you're going to start another one, Gus? What's wrong with it?

AUGUSTUS: Nothing. It's damned good.

MATTHEW: Well, then?

AUGUSTUS: (*Handing him the palette.*) Well then, it's your turn.

AUGUSTUS goes over to DORELIA who is standing by a seat with the necessary equipment AUGUSTUS needs for the picture, which he puts on. MATTHEW stands speechless still.

DORELIA: (*Looking across.*) All right, Matthew – off you go.

AUGUSTUS: (*Sitting, picking up his glass and raising it to DORELIA; quietly.*) To the success of Operation Dormouse.

CURTAIN.

ACT II

SCENE 1

Fryern Court, Hampshire. Spring, 1958

When the CURTAIN rises, DORELIA is sitting at the refectory table, crocheting. The doorbell rings.

DORELIA goes out to open the door.

MATTHEW SMITH comes in, looking a lot older than he did in the previous scene. He is followed by DORELIA. He puts down a small suitcase and turns to receive DORELIA's greeting.

DORELIA: Matthew. (*She embraces him.*)

MATTHEW: Dodo. Am I far too early?

DORELIA: No. You couldn't be.

MATTHEW: I caught an earlier train than I meant to. And the taxi-driver drove like Jehu. Where's Gus?

DORELIA: In the garden studio. He always is. Do sit down. Would you like some tea?

MATTHEW: No, thanks. I had a cup on the train.

DORELIA: A drink then?

MATTHEW: No, not yet.

DORELIA: Congratulations on your knighthood by the way.

MATTHEW: Thank you.

DORELIA: Matthew. I'd like to talk to you before Gus barges in and shouts me down. So can I start now?

MATTHEW: Why not?

DORELIA: Do you want to wash your hands or anything like that before I do?

MATTHEW: No thanks. I did that on the train too.

DORELIA: When did you last see Gus?

MATTHEW: Much too long ago. Last year? The year before? The year before that? Well, you don't come up to London much. And, anyway, I've been in France a lot.

DORELIA: When are you going next?

MATTHEW: Next month.

DORELIA: Would you take Gus?

MATTHEW: Yes, willingly. But would he want to go?

DORELIA: Yes, if you asked him.

MATTHEW: Certainly I will, then.

DORELIA: That's sweet of you. He's got bogged down here, you see. He fiddles round all day and half the night too with that bloody triptych. Had he started it when you were here last?

MATTHEW: Yes. I rather liked it. Although, I'm not sure I understood it.

DORELIA: Who does? Least of all him! Oh, he blathers on about it being allegorical, which hides a multitude of sins as you well know. But when it comes down to it, though I wouldn't dream of telling him this, it's not getting any better. In fact, it's a mess. Charles Wheeler wants to show it at the summer exhibition sometime, when he's got it right. But, Matthew, he'll never get it right. The only thing he's sure to do is make it worse. And I can't bear to see him slogging on at it. It'll kill me, if it doesn't kill him first.

MATTHEW: Poor Dodo.

DORELIA: So at least he'd get away from it, if you took him to France.

MATTHEW: And you'd get away from him.

DORELIA: And he'd get away from me. I get on his nerves, Matthew. That's another thing that worries me. I sometimes think I ought to go away and leave him.

MATTHEW: Don't do that.

DORELIA: I'm sorely tempted to. He's got so many children. Couldn't they look after him?

MATTHEW: No – not as well as you do.

DORELIA: Flatterer!

MATTHEW: No. Just observer.

DORELIA: He keeps saying that he can't paint any more.

MATTHEW: And is it true?

DORELIA: Yes, Matthew, I'm afraid it is – comparatively speaking with the past. If he'd take his portrait painting up again, he might be all right but, as I say, he's got bogged down on this triptych. What I want you to do, Matthew, is to get him back on portrait painting. Talk him into it when you're in France together.

MATTHEW: I'll try to.

DORELIA: After all, it's what he's best at, isn't it?

MATTHEW: He's certainly outstanding at it.

DORELIA: Yet he'll think up any excuse not to. For example, he took sculpture up a year or two back when Fiore came down here to do his bust. And he was quite good at it. But it didn't satisfy him and he gave up almost at once and then went back to his triptych. I think he thinks he's lost his touch for portrait painting in his old age.

MATTHEW: Old age. He's not eighty yet!

DORELIA: He will be next year.

MATTHEW: And I'm only a year younger.

DORELIA: What part of France are you going to?

MATTHEW: The South.

DORELIA: That's where you've done your best work, isn't it? How lovely.

MATTHEW: Any other orders, Dodo?

DORELIA: Yes, one. And the most important perhaps. Try and make him enjoy life again. Because he doesn't any more. Not for a moment. And it isn't just because he can't do all the things he used to. It's outside him. Or it should be. But it isn't. The fact is that ever since they dropped those bombs on Nagasaki and the other place he's got progressively more gloomy, worrying about the children and their children and the future of the world in general. He never used to be like that but since the last war ended, he's got more and more depressed. And I just don't know what to do about it, Matthew. I'm so sorry burdening you like this. I know I'm being selfish. But I'm desperate. And asking you to take him away with you is my only hope. Although I know it won't work.

MATTHEW: Why do you say that?

DORELIA: Because I know it won't. One can't talk people into doing things that they don't want to do. And are determined not to do.

MATTHEW: It worked with me. When you and Gus planned Operation Dormouse.

DORELIA: That's true.

MATTHEW: And I've never looked back since.

DORELIA: That's true, too. And you're talking much more than you used to. Why is that?

MATTHEW: Because I'm confident.

AUGUSTUS comes in.

AUGUSTUS: (*Advancing on him.*) Hullo there, Matthew.

MATTHEW: Hullo, Gus. How are you?

AUGUSTUS: Dodo's told you, hasn't she?

MATTHEW: Told me what?

AUGUSTUS: How I am.

MATTHEW: Oh yes, I see. Yes, I suppose she has.

DORELIA: I've just been pointing out to Matthew that he's talking much more than he used to.

AUGUSTUS: Watch it, Matthew, or you'll get like me.

DORELIA: He says it's due to having confidence.

MATTHEW: Which in its turn is due to you two.

AUGUSTUS: And you've never looked back, have you?

MATTHEW: That's exactly what I've just been telling Dodo.

AUGUSTUS: Not since we persuaded you to have a go at painting me – remember?

MATTHEW: Yes, of course I do, Gus.

AUGUSTUS: And a bloody awful picture it was. I don't mean the painting. I just mean that it made me look bloody awful. Like a randy old bull in a china shop. It's funny how a mousey little sod like you can come up with a great big bruising portrait like that, whereas mine of you was gentleness itself.

MATTHEW: Well, we had different models, that's how.

AUGUSTUS: Would you like to come and see my Sistine Chapel?

MATTHEW: No, thanks, Gus.

AUGUSTUS: Why not? Has she been telling you that it's a wash-out?

MATTHEW: No, of course not. But I'm tired after the journey. Anyway, it's getting dark. I'd like to see it in the morning.

AUGUSTUS: Very good, Sir Matthew. That was great, old fellow, that was. I've not seen you since it happened have I?

MATTHEW: I don't think so. But you wrote me a nice letter. Both of you did.

AUGUSTUS: Well, that was the least we could do. I used to wonder why they made you a knight, Matthew, and made me an OM.

MATTHEW: Because you're the more distinguished.

AUGUSTUS: No, I don't think it's that. Actually, the answer came to me just now, when I was standing staring at my triptych and remembered you were coming. The OM's for slogging plus a bit of merit so it doesn't really matter if the chap who gets it's a prize shit or not, whereas a knighthood, although it's for both of those as well, is also for good manners which I wouldn't qualify for.

DORELIA: You're talking nonsense, Gus.

AUGUSTUS: Has anyone had tea yet?

DORELIA: Not yet. Matthew had some on the train. We'll have it soon. But, first of all, there's something Matthew wants to ask you.

MATTHEW: That's right, Gus. I want to take you off to France next month.

AUGUSTUS: What part?

MATTHEW: To Villeneuve, Roquebrune, Menton.

AUGUSTUS: What for?

MATTHEW: For a holiday.

AUGUSTUS: She's just been telling you I need one, hasn't she?

MATTHEW: That's right.

AUGUSTUS: Because I've got the worst case of the glooms since Job.

MATTHEW: Yes.

AUGUSTUS: And that she's not certain which she's most browned off with – my triptych or me.

MATTHEW: That's right.

DORELIA: (*Not too warmly.*) I'll go and get your tea.

DORELIA goes.

AUGUSTUS: (*Looking after her ruefully.*) I take it the idea was meant to come from you.

MATTHEW: Yes, I suppose so. But life's too short for intrigue.

AUGUSTUS: (*Laughing.*) And anyway you're no Iago, are you? In fact, you're just about the most straightforward man I ever met.

MATTHEW: You flatter me.

AUGUSTUS: I'm just defining you. And you're the calmest. How you painted all those fiery nudes, I'll never know. The very idea makes one think of bank clerks writing rude things on the shit-house wall.

MATTHEW: You don't seem half so down as Dodo seems to think.

AUGUSTUS: You've cheered me up – that's why. When do we start?

MATTHEW: The third of April.

AUGUSTUS: How long for?

MATTHEW: Two or three months.

AUGUSTUS: What will we do?

MATTHEW: Sit in the sun, if there is any. And talk. And there'll be a Cézanne exhibition in Aix when we're there.

AUGUSTUS: I can't wait, Matthew. I've not been away for years. Except to Poppet down at Opio whenever Dodo thinks I've got myself into a tangle with some nubile teenager. Which isn't very often these days. Life's a bugger, Matthew, isn't it?

MATTHEW: Not if you make the most of it.

AUGUSTUS: I've always made the most of it – that's been my trouble.

MATTHEW: Well, why don't you go on doing just that?

AUGUSTUS: (A) because I can't – as far as women are concerned.

MATTHEW: I didn't mean that, Gus.

AUGUSTUS: (*Carrying straight on.*) And (b) because I'm too depressed.

MATTHEW: About nuclear weapons?

AUGUSTUS: Yes. She told you that as well.

MATTHEW: She did. You're not the only one, Gus.

AUGUSTUS: You're with me, are you?

MATTHEW: Yes, of course – who isn't?

AUGUSTUS: Why the devil don't they scrap them, then?

MATTHEW: Because they're scared.

AUGUSTUS: No more than I am. And I'm still for scrapping them. So why can't they be?

MATTHEW: Unilaterally?

AUGUSTUS: Of course. To set the other fellow an example.

MATTHEW: You're an optimist, Gus. And that doesn't go with your Job image.

AUGUSTUS: You're laughing at me.

MATTHEW: No, I'm not. I'm merely pinpointing your inconsistencies.

AUGUSTUS: I hope you won't be using long words like that in the South of France.

MATTHEW: I hope that I won't have to. Let's agree to drop the nuclear theme, shall we, when we're out there?

AUGUSTUS: I can't drop it, Matthew. That's my trouble. It gets me down. Every time I look out of the window at the apple blossom and the blue sky, I think "That'll be a desert one day when the bombs start falling". And there won't be anybody left alive, except a few unlucky ones who've burrowed underground like rabbits. And there won't be any paintbrushes or easels so that artists can immortalize the beauty that they see around them. Not that that'll matter as there won't be any beauty. There'll be nothing but a desert, Matthew. That's what gets me down.

MATTHEW: Let me repeat. You're not the only one, Gus.

AUGUSTUS: People ought to do something about it then.

MATTHEW: What can they do, if they don't trust the other fellow?

AUGUSTUS: Learn to trust him.

MATTHEW: Ah – but that takes time.

AUGUSTUS: There won't be time, if we don't watch it.

MATTHEW: We are watching it, I like to think, Gus.

AUGUSTUS: What's the matter with you? You're not talking like an artist. You're talking like a bloody politician. Weighing this and weighing that regardless of the immorality of the whole exercise.

MATTHEW: The world's not run on morals.

AUGUSTUS: Then it damned well should be.

MATTHEW: But it isn't, Gus. And, if it was, I can't help wondering if you would have enjoyed it much.

AUGUSTUS: (*Ignoring this quip.*) It's artists who have got to do it, Matthew. Can't you see that? No one else is going to. And if artists like you argue the toss, then there's no hope – none whatever.

MATTHEW: Yes. There is. There's always hope.

AUGUSTUS: You didn't think that when you packed it in.

MATTHEW: Agreed. But it was there, Gus. I just couldn't see it. You and Dodo gave it back to me.

DORELIA comes in with the tea.

AUGUSTUS: He can't stop talking, Dodo. What's come over him? He never used to say a bloody word!

DORELIA: He never had a chance when you were on full flood, Gus.

AUGUSTUS: That damned knighthood's done it, bloody old snob that he is!

DORELIA: Milk, Matthew?

MATTHEW: Yes, please.

AUGUSTUS: We're starting on the third of April, Dodo. I'm so damned excited. I can't sit still.

DORELIA: (*Giving him his tea cup.*) Well, be careful.

He turns away and starts walking round with his tea cup.

Well done, Matthew.

AUGUSTUS: (*Swinging round again with the tea cup.*) What else did you tell him to do?

DORELIA: Nothing, I don't think.

AUGUSTUS: You did. I see it in your eye. I know – to get me back on portrait painting. (*To MATTHEW.*) Didn't she?

MATTHEW: She did.

AUGUSTUS: I don't know what she means. I'm always painting bloody portraits. (*To DORELIA.*) What more do you want?

DORELIA: A lot, Gus.

AUGUSTUS: Well, there's de la Mare, Charles Morgan, Schweitzer still outstanding. Who else? Ah, yes, Cecil Beaton.

DORELIA: And you'll never do them if you can find half an excuse not to.

AUGUSTUS: Half – I've got a whole one! A damned good one too. I'm no damn good at it, not any more.

DORELIA: That's not true, Gus.

AUGUSTUS: It is true. And I'll bet you told him so. I can't paint. I'm an old man, Matthew. And a pissed-up old man, to boot.

DORELIA: You see, Matthew, what you've got to deal with. But I'm trusting you to get him started again.

AUGUSTUS: He'll have a job. (*He swings round with his tea cup again.*) And I'll tell you something else, young fellow. If you do suborn me and I get through that lot, I'll be in my dotage by the time I get to Cecil. Still if it makes Dodo happy I suppose it'll all be worthwhile.

DORELIA hands MATTHEW his hat.

Do you think I'll ever get to Cecil, Dodo?

DORELIA: Yes, of course you will, Gus. (*She looks at the transformed MATTHEW.*)

Blackout.

SCENE 2

The same. 1960.

The Lights come up on AUGUSTUS painting CECIL BEATON. Silence. AUGUSTUS's head is shaking and his beret falls off at intervals. He pauses and starts looking at the picture in despair. He attempts another brush stroke, hates it, and starts again, his hand shaking worse than ever.

AUGUSTUS: Did you know Matthew Smith?

CECIL: No.

AUGUSTUS: He died last September.

CECIL: So I saw.

AUGUSTUS: We shared a final holiday. When was it? Last year. Or the year before it could have been. The last good picture that I painted was of him. At the end of the war. You ever see it?

CECIL: Yes.

AUGUSTUS: What did you think of it?

CECIL: I liked it.

AUGUSTUS: You'll be lucky if you like this.

CECIL: Nonsense.

AUGUSTUS: Something tells me that it's going to be a stinker. Well, what else can you expect. I'm past it. (*He walks towards CECIL waving his paintbrush.*) Did you hear what I said, Cecil?

CECIL: Yes. That time. And every other time you've said it in the last two days.

AUGUSTUS: I'm sorry. But it's true. Poor Matthew tried to get me going again on that holiday, but even he soon realized that he was flogging a dead horse.

CECIL: Why don't we have a break now for elevenses, Gus?

AUGUSTUS: Not if you're going to America next week.

CECIL: What does that matter? Don't be silly. I've already promised I'll go on sitting for you when I get back.

AUGUSTUS: I'll be dead when you get back!

CECIL: What nonsense!

AUGUSTUS: (*Stopping work again.*) Are you going to marry Garbo when you get out there?

CECIL: Good heavens, no. She wants to be alone!

AUGUSTUS: Well, you've got that in common, haven't you – as far as women are concerned.

CECIL: I wouldn't say that.

He paints on.

AUGUSTUS: (*Stopping again.*) Who does all the talking when you're alone together?

CECIL: Who do you think? Me, of course. Except when I'm struck dumb in admiration of her beauty, which is almost all the time.

AUGUSTUS: She's a good-looking woman, I'll give her that.

CECIL: God gave her that before you did, Gus.

AUGUSTUS: Well, I'm happy to endorse it. And I'm glad you introduced us to each other.

CECIL: But you didn't want to paint her.

AUGUSTUS: No.

CECIL: Why not?

AUGUSTUS: For the same reason that I didn't want to go to bed with her. Or maybe, I did want to. But for an experiment. Not for pleasure. Just to see if I'd survive the night without a touch of frostbite.

CECIL: You misunderstand her, Gus, she's got a warm heart.

AUGUSTUS: Like a thermos with hot coffee in it! I daresay she has. But she's not letting anyone unscrew the top. So, *ipso facto*, she's not letting anyone screw her.

CECIL: Must you be so fucking crude – it shocks me to the core.

AUGUSTUS: Oh, no – it doesn't. You pretend it does, that's all. Because it's your pose. But you don't deceive me. You're as prim as an old spinster outwardly. But underneath you've got the mind and the vocabulary of a sergeant major! (*Another short resumption of work, and then another pause for conversation.*) You're a strange man, Cecil. But I can't help liking you.

CECIL: I like you too, though God knows why!

AUGUSTUS: (*Ignoring this.*) It's funny that I should. Because you're not my type at all. In fact, I doubt if there's two men – if I can use that word about you – on this entire planet who're more different. You're an aesthete, you're precious, you're in love with yourself.

CECIL: (*Cutting in.*) And with Garbo.

AUGUSTUS: Mentally, I dare say. In the same way as a soldier sticks a pin-up of her on the wall behind his bunk and then indulges himself later underneath the blankets after lights out.

CECIL: You're being crude again.

AUGUSTUS: I'm being analytical. I'm trying to assess the depth of your devotion to this woman.

CECIL: You're much too superficial to succeed in doing that, Gus. You can't help it of course. You're a child of nature – lacking all refinement. No relationship means anything to you unless it's physical. Not even now, when you're past it. That's why you're so lonely and so desperate. Because you can't make contact any more. You're like a dead bulb in a table lamp. And it's too dark. And far too late at night to change it.

AUGUSTUS: That's true, Cecil. That's the truest thing I ever heard you say. And, by God, it's the cruellest.

CECIL: Sorry, but you needled me, Gus.

AUGUSTUS: Well, you've got your own back now.

CECIL: Why don't we get on with the sitting?

AUGUSTUS: Because I can't paint – that's why.

CECIL: Of course you can. You're painting just as well as ever. Don't be so defeatist.

AUGUSTUS: I'm not, Cecil. The spark's gone, as you just said. I can't make contact any more. I'm like an old rogue elephant who knows his number's up, the only difference being that he'll disappear into the bush and fade out like a gentleman, while I'll be stuffed into a hearse and planted in the cemetery at Fordingbridge! And you'll come back here with Dodo and whatever of my countless offspring wants a free drink. And you'll say to one another, "Thank God that old bugger's gone. Because he's been a burden to us all for far too long." And nobody'll thank God more than Dodo will.

CECIL: Don't be so bloody morbid, Gus – for God's sake. You're talking like a drunk talks to a policeman when the level of his whisky intake's lapping at his eyeballs. The light's still there, Gus, and if you'd only give up dousing it with cheap red wine, it'd shine as bright as ever.

AUGUSTUS: Rot! I'm over eighty and it's bloody fused. And there's no electrician on this earth, nor any God in Heaven, who can fit me out with a replacement. So I can't see any more. I can't see what I'm looking for. I'm in the dark. And artists can't paint in the dark. And don't quote Milton at me. Because Milton was a poet. And a poet doesn't need eyes, although they're a help. But he can do without them at a pinch. Because his mind's his chief requirement. But an artist needs his eyes. And he needs light if he's to use them. And he might as well be dead when (*Imitating CECIL.*) "the bulb's fused and it's too late to change it".

CECIL: Sorry, Gus. I didn't mean to hurt you. But you needled me when you cast doubts on my devotion to a certain lady.

AUGUSTUS: So we're back on Garbo, are we?

CECIL: Well, why not? It's better than a morbid monologue from you.

AUGUSTUS: And have you ever been on Garbo, Cecil, in the biblical sense?

CECIL: As if I'd tell you.

AUGUSTUS: You don't have to tell me. Any more than you need tell me that I need another drink. Because it's obvious. Have one yourself.

CECIL: Well, just a little sip.

AUGUSTUS: A little sip! Hark at you! Poor old Cecil.

CECIL: What's so poor about me?

AUGUSTUS: Just a little sip – that ought to be your epitaph. "He flitted like a dainty bee from flower to flower and took a little sip of everything. But never drank sufficient of the rich red wine of life to lubricate his manhood."

He hands him a full glass.

Try it, Cecil. Now. Drink deep. And see if we can make a man of you before it's too late.

CECIL takes a sip.

Go on. Drain it to the last drop.

He does.

Well done. How do you feel now?

CECIL: The same as ever. Happy in my impotence!

AUGUSTUS: (*Roaring with laughter.*) That's funny, Cecil. Happy in your impotence. That's funny.

CECIL: Thank you. I thought you'd like it, and I also thought I'd say it before you did.

AUGUSTUS: You're a strange man, Cecil. Or a half-man, rather.

CECIL: You've already said that.

AUGUSTUS: Have I told you that I like you?

CECIL: Yes. You did just now. And I returned the compliment.

AUGUSTUS: And then attempted to destroy me.

CECIL: You're indestructible. So never worry. Anyway you irritated me beyond endurance.

AUGUSTUS: Did I? What did I say?

CECIL: Don't remind me, please.

AUGUSTUS: Yes, Garbo – I remember. I annoyed you about Garbo. What did I say?

CECIL: Never mind – let's drop the subject.

AUGUSTUS: Not before we've drunk a toast to her. Your glass is empty. (*He starts to refill it.*)

CECIL: That's enough.

AUGUSTUS: (*Raising his.*) To Garbo.

CECIL: Garbo.

AUGUSTUS: Coupled with your happy impotence!

Abandoning the toast, CECIL gets up and puts down his glass.

What's up?

CECIL: I just find you a bore this morning, that's all, Gus. I'll see you when I get back from America.

AUGUSTUS: No, don't go.

CECIL: Why not? What's the point of staying? You're not painting me. You're just insulting me.

AUGUSTUS: It was your crack about your happy impotence. Not mine. I just repeated it. Sit down. I'm going to paint you now.

CECIL: You're in no condition to.

AUGUSTUS: I'm perfectly all right. I've painted better men than you in a worse state than this. So go and sit down.

CECIL: All right, Gus. But just be careful what you say. Or I'll bugger straight off.

AUGUSTUS: Please yourself. (*He stands looking fixedly at CECIL.*)

CECIL: Stop staring at me, Gus, for God's sake. And get on with it.

AUGUSTUS: Shut up. I'm only looking at you. Trying to find out if there's still something in your face that God supplied you with that hasn't been negated by Max Factor! Anyway, what's wrong with you. A cat can look at a king, can't he; and there's nothing in the rules that says he can't look at a queen.

CECIL: One more crack like that, Gus – and I'll –

AUGUSTUS: Bugger off, I know. But you won't. You're far too vain – so shut up. Anyway I was just joking. (*He starts painting.*)

CECIL: (*After a while.*) Do you know what you remind me of, Gus?

AUGUSTUS: No. And I don't want to.

CECIL: Well, I'll tell you. It's too good to keep to myself. You're like a drunk in a pub trying to play darts with a long knitting needle he's forgotten to leave go of.

AUGUSTUS: (*Throwing down his brush.*) OK. If you're so bloody clever, you can paint your own damned portrait. I'm not going to!

He moves forward towards CECIL, who remains impassive.

(*Bellowing.*) Do you hear me, Cecil? I'm not going to.

CECIL: Don't shout at me, Gus. And pick that paintbrush up. I'm paying for the bloody thing. So get on with it.

AUGUSTUS: Not unless you take back what you said just now.

CECIL: It was a joke, Gus.

AUGUSTUS: I dare say. And so was mine about cats looking at queens. But you didn't like it, did you?

CECIL: Not much. But I didn't ask you to withdraw it.

AUGUSTUS: Well, I'm asking you to withdraw yours.

CECIL: All right. If you'll get on with it.

AUGUSTUS: I'll get on with it.

CECIL: All right, withdrawn.

AUGUSTUS picks up the brush, goes back to his easel and starts painting again. There is silence then CECIL, spoiling for another quarrel, starts again.

You're worse than a spoilt baby, aren't you, Gus?

AUGUSTUS: I'm not a baby. I'm an artist – trying to do his job.

CECIL: And damned badly.

AUGUSTUS: All right go to someone else, if you don't like it. But, for God's sake take your make-up off before you do. It'll make things easier for the poor devil!

CECIL rises in his seat with a view to going.

Sit down.

CECIL hesitates.

(*Bellowing.*) Sit down. Don't be such a baby, Cecil.

CECIL does and the session resumes again. And again, after a pause, CECIL has another go.

CECIL: You're a bully, Gus. That's what you are. A baby. And a bully. And you've been one all your life.

AUGUSTUS: (*So far unruffled.*) And what have you been, except bloody impotent?

CECIL: Well, if I have, thank God for it! Because it's saved me having on my conscience anything as burdensome as you must carry on yours – if you've got one.

AUGUSTUS: Mine's quite clear, thanks.

CECIL: Then you can't have got one.

AUGUSTUS: What does that mean?

CECIL: It means you've done what you wanted when you wanted all your life and got away with it unlike some of the people that you've done it to. And do you give a damn!

AUGUSTUS: What people?

CECIL: Ida for one.

AUGUSTUS: Don't you dare say that!

CECIL: Why not, Gus? Everybody else does. That's why I prefer my impotence. When I think of poor lovely gentle little Ida – with her oval face and straight eyes.

AUGUSTUS: Shut up, Cecil.

CECIL: (*Going on.*) So you've got a conscience after all. Poor little Ida lying in a hospital in Paris with a drunken husband sitting by her bed and knowing he'll be back in Dodo's arms before the hospital had signed her death certificate.

AUGUSTUS, without a word, goes out of the room with lowered head.

CECIL, regretful rather, sits there looking after him, then gets up and walks round the canvas to look at the portrait.

DORELIA comes in with coffee.

DORELIA: Hello, Cecil.

CECIL: Hello, Dodo. (*He kisses her.*)

DORELIA: What have you been doing to Augustus?

CECIL: We've been quarrelling.

DORELIA: Who started it?

CECIL: He did. He mocked me about Garbo.

DORELIA: He was teasing you, I'm sure.

CECIL: And then he made a crack about Max Factor and it got my goat. So I cracked back and then he shouted at me. So I told him not to bully me.

DORELIA: It all sounds very childish.

CECIL: It was up till then. But then I told him that he should have Ida on his conscience.

DORELIA: That was unkind.

CECIL: I know, Dodo. And I'm very sorry.

DORELIA: Do you want to go?

CECIL: Unless you want me to stay.

DORELIA: Please do. Milk?

CECIL: Please.

DORELIA: Sugar?

CECIL: No thanks, Dodo.

DORELIA: (*Taking his empty glass and giving him the coffee.*) What a pity that you quarrelled.

CECIL: Never mind. We'll make it up in no time.

DORELIA: I don't think there's much time left. At least, I hope not.

CECIL: Don't say that.

DORELIA: Why not? It's what I pray for every night. He thinks he can't paint any more.

CECIL: That's what he told me. But I don't believe it.

DORELIA: Nonetheless, it's true. So what else can he do? Except die. In the old days when his inspiration failed him, he consoled himself with women. Any woman. Ida – or me, or his current model. Or the last one. Or the next one – or all three at once. But that's all finished now, too. So he doesn't want to go on living.

CECIL: He's not told me that.

DORELIA: He's told me.

CECIL: Only when he's drunk, I'm sure.

DORELIA: That's when he speaks the truth. He's much too shy to speak it when he's sober. So he only speaks it when he's drunk. And that's what he says. Day in day out – till it nearly drives me mad.

CECIL: I'm sorry, Dodo. How I wish that I could help.

DORELIA: No one can, Cecil. Except him. If he could only face the facts and just live out the rest of his existence like a normal person. But he isn't normal, Cecil, that's the trouble,

CECIL: Who is, Dodo, when you think about it.

DORELIA: I am, Cecil – but then I'm a woman. And a woman doesn't despair.

CECIL: Ida being the exception.

DORELIA: Ida didn't despair. Anyway, why bring her up?

CECIL: Because she's on my mind. She had a raw deal – wouldn't you agree?

DORELIA: No. If I did, I couldn't live with myself.

CECIL: But you took him off her.

DORELIA: Took him off her, Cecil! I took Gus off Ida! Don't be silly. Everyone took Gus off Ida. Every model that he ever had who wasn't wearing trousers. So why blame me?

CECIL: Because you stayed with him.

DORELIA: *(Patiently.)* Cecil, Ida had no jealousy.

CECIL: How do you know?

DORELIA: Because she loved me. And she never wanted me to be unfaithful never – to Gus or to her. She was supremely happy, Cecil. But I don't expect you to believe me.

CECIL: I'm beginning to – I must confess. You're most convincing.

DORELIA: That's because I'm passionate about it.

CECIL: And not guilty.

DORELIA: And not guilty, Cecil.

CECIL: Case dismissed. If he's not coming back I'm going.

DORELIA: Don't go, Cecil. You're his last sitter.

CECIL: That's a gloomy statement, if I ever heard one.

DORELIA: It's true though. *(She walks round and stands looking at the canvas.)*

CECIL: It's a bugger, isn't it?

DORELIA: He'll get it right.

CECIL: You'll go to Heaven, Dodo.

DORELIA: Must I, Cecil?

CECIL: But I doubt if Gus will. They're not that broad-minded, surely!

DORELIA: Certainly they are.

CECIL: I stand corrected.

DORELIA: Jesus loved the drop-outs.

CECIL: I daresay. But Gus is not a drop-out, is he? He's an OM.

DORELIA: And he doesn't give a damn about it.

CECIL: Yes, he does. He's pleased as Punch about it.

DORELIA: But he doesn't flaunt it, does he?

CECIL: No – I'll give him that.

DORELIA: Well, that's what Jesus doesn't like. So he'll be OK, won't he?

CECIL: If you say so, Dodo. (*Smiling.*) For a non-believer, you seem very well briefed.

DORELIA: I don't like you. You're being cynical.

CECIL: I'm not. I'm cheering you up, that's all.

DORELIA: In a thoroughly facetious manner.

CECIL: Never mind the manner. Hang on to the therapy!

AUGUSTUS comes in again with a bottle in his hand.

AUGUSTUS: Right. Action stations! You've been entertaining Cecil – have you, Dodo – in my absence?

DORELIA: He's been entertaining me, Gus.

AUGUSTUS: You're a good girl. You're both good girls! (*He turns to* CECIL.) I'm sorry, Cecil. But I thought I ought to have a little lie-down. I felt shaky on my pins just now. And so I thought I ought to have a little lie-down. Ever since I had my prostate done, I like to have a little lie-down when I can. I always liked a little lie-down, actually, before I had my prostate done. But not for the same reasons. (*He starts fiddling with his painting equipment.*) Cecil.

CECIL: Yes, Gus?

AUGUSTUS: Did we have a row before I went to have my lie-down?

CECIL: Yes, Gus.

AUGUSTUS: What about?

CECIL: A fellow playing darts with a long knitting-needle.

AUGUSTUS: Ah, yes, I remember. Well, let's shake hands on it and forget it.

They shake hands.

CECIL: It's forgotten.

Satisfied they've made things up, DORELIA *starts to go out.*

AUGUSTUS: Hold it, Dodo. Are you staying to lunch, Cecil?

CECIL: No, I've got a date at one. I'm sorry.

AUGUSTUS: Never mind. We'll try again another day.

DORELIA: (*From the door.*) What time do you want lunch, Gus?

AUGUSTUS: One o'clock tomorrow. I'm not eating any more today.

DORELIA goes.

She doesn't like me drinking. But I have to to forget the world. When I opened my eyes just now, I thought, "By God, you're still there, are you, you pissed-up old bastard! – spinning madly to destruction just like you were when I shut them." Then I thought, "I can't keep poor old Cecil waiting any longer." And so I took another swig and came back in. I find life unendurable, don't you?

CECIL: Not quite.

AUGUSTUS: Then you're lucky.

CECIL: And so are you, I would have thought – with Dodo to look after you.

AUGUSTUS: It isn't Dodo I find unendurable. Except sometimes, when she gets on my nerves. And that's inevitable, as I'm not the kind of man who ought to have a woman as a permanent attachment. That's because I'm not a bloody hoarder. When I've emptied this damned bottle – I won't keep it, will I? What's the point, it's dead. I'll get another one that's full. And when I've emptied that, I'll get another one. And so on. That's the way it used to be with women in the old days – but it isn't any longer. All that I can manage now is uncork the occasional half-bottle when I get a model who's sufficiently besotted to survive the operation. Otherwise, I've got to settle for the empties – one of which is Dodo. So I can't paint, and I can't screw. But that isn't why I drink. I'll tell you something, Cecil, that you never would have guessed, not in a thousand years. I drink to keep the Third World War at bay. That's what I'm trying to forget. Not nineteen fourteen or the last one. But the next one. That's the one I'm trying to forget before it happens. I became a conchie back in nineteen forty-four when I was painting Monty – stop me if I've told you this before.

CECIL: You haven't, Gus.

AUGUSTUS: He brought a young staff officer along with him who died exactly three months later on the Second Front. I can still see him, Cecil, when I called him back to say goodbye as they were leaving, and I shook his hand. I told him I'd paint him when he came on leave in six months' time; although I knew damned well he never would. And so did Dodo. Dodo's like a gypsy. She's on speaking terms with death. She's got a gypsy's instinct. That was why I never had a moment's worry about Caspar during the whole war. Because she never cried when he went off to sea. But what about the next time, Cecil? What about the little Caspars who are everybody else's children. And their sisters? And their children? They'll all be dead as mutton in a matter of ten minutes. The whole damned lot, wiped out in a jiffy. That's why someone's got to stop the bloody thing. That's why I've been in touch with Bertrand Russell and I'm going to a meeting with him in Trafalgar Square next month.

CECIL: You're not!

AUGUSTUS: I am – so put that where the monkey put the nuts.

CECIL: But he's a crackpot, Gus.

AUGUSTUS: So what! We're going to need a crackpot to crack all the other crackpots on the head before it's too late, aren't we? Come on, let's get going. You're talking too much. (*He goes over to his palette and then comes back to CECIL.*) I'll tell you what's wrong with our bloody set-up, Cecil. Man's not up to it. And no one less so than the bloody politicians, They're always on about morality. And what the other fellow's doing wrong. But do they ever stop to take a look at themselves? Not them! That's no way to run a bloody planet, Cecil. Not unless you want it to disintegrate. So what's the answer – Bertrand Russell's for my money. Get rid of the bloody weapons. Jesus thought of it two thousand years ago. Well, didn't he? He said, "put up your sword."

CECIL: Yes, but he didn't say get rid of it. Well, not until the other fellow has got rid of his, at any rate. It's always sensible to carry an umbrella, when it looks like rain.

AUGUSTUS: Rain! God Almighty, rain! You call it rain!

CECIL: It's just an illustration.

AUGUSTUS: And a bloody silly one. OK. Let's say the world puts up its sword. Right?

CECIL: Right.

AUGUSTUS: That's the first step to scrapping it, then, isn't it?

CECIL: Perhaps.

AUGUSTUS: In that case let's drink to them both. You haven't got a glass.

CECIL: No, Dodo took it.

AUGUSTUS: Which would you prefer? The bottle or my glass?

CECIL: The bottle.

AUGUSTUS: I've been drinking out of it as well.

CECIL: Oh, have you?

AUGUSTUS: You're a nervous old thing, aren't you, Cecil. Come on! What's the matter. Do you think I've got VD or something?

CECIL: No, I just like clean things.

AUGUSTUS: Well, I'm clean.

CECIL: I'm sure you are.

AUGUSTUS: It may surprise you. Just as it surprises me. I must have had a charmed life. (*He cleans the bottle neck with his beard.*) There, the bottle's clean as well now. (*He hands it to CECIL.*)

CECIL: Thank you.

AUGUSTUS turns away to pick up his own glass and CECIL takes the opportunity of cleaning the bottle neck with a handkerchief.

AUGUSTUS: Right. (*Raising his glass.*) To Jesus Christ and Bertrand Russell.

CECIL: (*Raising the bottle.*) Jesus Christ and Bertrand Russell. (*He takes a swig, then raises the bottle again.*) And to the world putting up its sword.

AUGUSTUS: And I could tell it where to put it! (*He takes the bottle from CECIL.*)

Blackout.

SCENE 3

The same. Some months later.

It is the last sitting with CECIL BEATON. *The Lights come up on* AUGUSTUS *lunging at the canvas, dressed in beret, woollen denims and sweater.* CECIL *is watching, exquisitely posed.*

AUGUSTUS stops for a prolonged look at his work. He is well stoked up.

AUGUSTUS: Did Garbo send me her love?

CECIL: Yes, of course she did, Gus.

AUGUSTUS: And did you make base this time?

CECIL: Don't be so crude.

AUGUSTUS: Did you, Cecil?

CECIL: Never you mind.

AUGUSTUS: Do you know, I wouldn't put it past you. You look different, Cecil. There's a new look to you. What's the word I want? Monarchical. That's it. That's what you're looking. I'd better watch it or I'll start thinking I'm Landseer! (*After a pause.*) This is going to be the best I've ever painted, Cecil.

CECIL: Good for you, Gus.

AUGUSTUS paints on for a bit.

AUGUSTUS: I feel like a drink now. Like one?

CECIL: No, thanks, Gus.

AUGUSTUS: Well, I would. (*He fills his mug shakily.*)

CECIL: What have you been up to while I've been away?

AUGUSTUS: Damn all.

CECIL: You have. I read about it in the paper. In *The New York Times.* It said you'd been supporting Bertrand Russell in Trafalgar Square.

AUGUSTUS: That's right. He had a meeting there. And I was in the Gallery. And so I tottered down the steps and went across the road and sat beside him on the platform. Did they have a photograph?

CECIL: They did.

AUGUSTUS: What did I look like?

CECIL: An old tramp on methylated spirits!

AUGUSTUS: That's what Dodo said, more or less.

CECIL: Did it make you happy, Gus?

AUGUSTUS: What?

CECIL: Lending your support to that old crank.

AUGUSTUS: Yes. So don't try to argue with me like you did the last time you were here. I've got my ideas and you've got yours. And God, when He's got the time, will judge between us. And then act accordingly.

CECIL: By sending me to hell you mean.

AUGUSTUS: It's not for me to make His judgements for Him.

CECIL: I'll be all right. I'll tell Him peace through strength has always been my motto.

AUGUSTUS: And I'll tell Him peace and common sense has always been mine.

CECIL: Only since you fell in love with Monty's ADC.

AUGUSTUS: That's right. I stand corrected. I was arguing with G.B.S. just like you were just now. And he said I'd come round to his point of view when I was as mature as he was! That's what he said, Cecil. Then he said, "Think of me when you do." (*He shakes his head in wonderment.*) He'll be up there all right now.

CECIL: And do you think you'll be allowed to join him.

AUGUSTUS: If God's got His head screwed on right, He'll let me. And He'll send you down below and pour a glass of nectar out for me. And we'll sit and drink to your damnation. I can't wait to hear the cork pop, Cecil. I just hope He's got it in the fridge already as it won't be long now.

CECIL: Nonsense, Gus. You'll last forever.

AUGUSTUS: Not here, Cecil. There, maybe. But not here. And I won't be sorry. I've done all the good or harm that I was meant to do here. I expect you think the harm outweighs the good but maybe He won't, not if He's got a good eye for painting! (*He goes back to look at the canvas, fiddles with it for a bit.*) Come and have a look now, Cecil.

CECIL gets up and goes over.

CECIL: It's good. It's damned good.

AUGUSTUS: Yes, it's the best I've ever painted.

CECIL: Is it finished?

AUGUSTUS: What do you think?

CECIL: I think it is.

AUGUSTUS: What about a little touch up on that left eye?

CECIL: No, it's all right.

AUGUSTUS: You're afraid I'll bugger it up, aren't you?

CECIL: No, of course not.

AUGUSTUS: I am. I'm scared stiff. I can't paint the way I used to, you know.

CECIL: Nonsense.

AUGUSTUS: It's not nonsense. It's the truth. Each time I touch the bloody thing, I wreck it.

CECIL: Then don't touch it.

AUGUSTUS: (*Making for the door.*) I'll get Dodo and see what she thinks.

AUGUSTUS goes.

CECIL continues studying the canvas.

AUGUSTUS comes back with DORELIA.

Dodo, it's the best I've ever painted.

DORELIA: Wait until I've seen it.

AUGUSTUS: Cecil thinks so. Don't you, Cecil?

CECIL: Yes. I'm bound to say I do, Gus. Now I've had a second look.

DORELIA stands looking at the portrait in silence.

AUGUSTUS: You mean you didn't like it at first?

CECIL: It grows on you.

AUGUSTUS: But you said it was good, Cecil. You said it was damned good.

CECIL: And I meant it. But that didn't mean I thought it was the best that you'd ever painted. But I do now.

AUGUSTUS: What do you think, Dodo?

DORELIA: It's the best you've ever painted, Gus.

AUGUSTUS: You mean that, do you?

DORELIA: Yes.

AUGUSTUS: You really mean it?

DORELIA: Yes. Don't be so modest. What's come over you?

AUGUSTUS: I just don't know. I don't know any more.

DORELIA: Well, we do – don't we, Cecil?

CECIL: We do, Dodo. It's the best you've ever painted, Gus, by far.

AUGUSTUS: Then I'll go and get a bottle.

AUGUSTUS toddles off to get it.

DORELIA kisses CECIL and they stand together, silent, hugging one another. Then they separate and look back at the canvas.

CECIL: It's good, isn't it?

DORELIA: Yes, Cecil.

CECIL: But it's not the best he's ever painted.

DORELIA: No, not by a long way.

CECIL: But you said it was.

DORELIA: I know I did. To please him. So did you.

CECIL: But it is good.

DORELIA: Yes, Cecil. But not damned good.

CECIL: I said that to please him, too.

DORELIA: I know you did. And thank you.

The old man comes back with the champagne and three glasses on a tray. He looks about to drop it.

Let me take it, Gus.

AUGUSTUS: I'm all right, woman.

DORELIA: You sit down. And I'll open it.

He does, fumbling it.

AUGUSTUS: She fusses me. She's like a bloody nursemaid, Cecil. Once upon a time she was a fairy, dancing in the moonlight. Now she's nothing but a bloody nursemaid.

DORELIA: Just as well I am. A fairy would have pushed off long ago, you old curmudgeon.

AUGUSTUS: Listen to her!

DORELIA: Why should Cecil listen to me? You're the one that ought to listen.

CECIL: You'd never leave him, would you?

DORELIA: Don't be too sure.

Pop of the champagne cork.

AUGUSTUS: Where'll you hang it, Cecil?

CECIL: In the place of honour, naturally.

AUGUSTUS: And where's that? In the shit-house?!

CECIL: No, of course not. I'll have to see. I'll have to see where it looks best.

AUGUSTUS: I'll let you know the moment that it's finished.

CECIL: I'll look forward to that.

DORELIA: Cecil.

CECIL: (*Taking his champagne.*) Thank you.

DORELIA: (*Giving AUGUSTUS his glass.*) Gus.

AUGUSTUS: That's yours. (*He goes to fill his mug. To DORELIA.*) Right – you propose the toast.

DORELIA: (*Turning round and raising the glass.*) To Cecil. And his picture.

AUGUSTUS: Cecil and his picture.

CECIL: Gus and Dodo.

DORELIA: Gus and –

AUGUSTUS: (*Before she can finish.*) Ida.

DORELIA puts down her glass and runs out.

What's the matter?

CECIL: You just called her Ida.

AUGUSTUS: Oh, is that all? I've been doing that for fifty-eight years off and on when I've had one too many – you'd have thought she would've got used to it by now. (*He looks after her.*) Fifty-eight years, Cecil – fifty-eight years. It was in Holborn. She was in a black hat. And I passed her. And then looked back. And she looked back, too. And that was it. Your glass is empty.

CECIL: I'm all right.

AUGUSTUS: Well, I'm not. (*He gets up to refill his mug. Standing over him with the bottle.*) Come on.

CECIL: All right. Half a glass.

AUGUSTUS: Why half a glass? Why not a whole glass?

CECIL: Because I don't feel like it.

AUGUSTUS: You will after you've drunk it. Fifty-eight years. That's a long time. (*He refills it and returns to his seat, topping up his mug on the way, and still holding the bottle.*) She's a bloody jailor, Cecil.

CECIL: You can't do without her, Gus.

AUGUSTUS: I daresay not. I can't do with her either! I want freedom, Cecil. And I can't work when I haven't got it. (*He stares ahead for a while, then looks up into the distance.*) Do you know what I'd do if I was young enough to do it, Cecil?

CECIL: I could make a guess, Gus.

AUGUSTUS: (*Refilling his mug.*) I'd go off to the gypsies like I used to. I'd go off to the gypsies. And I'd eat a pheasant or a hare for supper that the local squire would never miss. And I'd sing the songs we used to sing together round the fire. And I'd kiss their wives and black-eyed children like I used to when the world and I were young. And I'd sleep beneath the moon with some young creature who'd never bruised the soles of her feet on a city pavement. And I'd wake to the dawn chorus and the rising sun to meet a fresh day. And we'd look at one another and see beauty, newly woken in each other's eyes and in each other's bodies. And we'd know what freedom was and what God made the world for. (*He sits silent and still.*)

CECIL: (*Getting up.*) Gus. Gus.

AUGUSTUS: Sorry, I was dreaming.

CECIL: Come on, Gus.

AUGUSTUS: Where to?

CECIL: Get up. I'll give you a hand.

AUGUSTUS: No, thanks. I'll be in this position soon for keeps and so I may as well get used to it.

CECIL: I must go or I'll be late for lunch.

AUGUSTUS: I'm sorry to have kept you.

CECIL: That's all right. I'll be in good time. Say goodbye to Dodo for me.

AUGUSTUS: You'll find her next door.

CECIL: All right. I'll pop in there on my way out. Goodbye, Gus. Thank you for the picture. I'll look forward to it. I'll look forward to the picture.

AUGUSTUS: (*Registering.*) It's my last, I reckon, Cecil.

CECIL: Nonsense.

AUGUSTUS: Dodo thinks so. I can see it in her eyes. Hi. Do you really like it, Cecil?

CECIL: Thank you for the honour, Gus.

Blackout.

AUGUSTUS and CECIL exit.

The Lights come up again.

DORELIA comes in, dressed in black and carrying a bunch of white flowers. She closes AUGUSTUS's painting box and looks round.

CECIL enters, also in black.

CECIL: Dodo, I stayed behind to thank you for the picture. It arrived two days ago.

DORELIA: Where are you going to hang it?

CECIL: Not where Gus suggested!

There is the sound of cars starting up and moving away.

DORELIA: (*Looking out of the window at the departing guests.*) Weren't they a funny crowd.

CECIL: Bizarre's the word I'd use.

DORELIA: Gus would have loved it though. With all those pretty models.

CECIL: And a lot of not so pretty art students.

DORELIA: He would have loved them too. And he'd have loved the gypsies most of all.

CECIL: Of course.

DORELIA: (*Turning from the window.*) I'm not so sure about the clergyman. He might have irritated him. He looked a bit bewildered.

CECIL: Can you blame him! He could never have thought up that congregation in his wildest dreams – not even after swigging half a dozen bottles of communion wine at a sitting!

DORELIA: (*Moving towards a chair.*) Cecil, don't be naughty. (*She sits.*) I can see what you mean though. It must have been an ordeal for him.

CECIL: And for you.

There is a pause. DORELIA looks up again at him.

DORELIA: But not for you.

CECIL: No. I'm too cynical.

DORELIA: About death?

CECIL: No, about life. Or the living, rather. I was watching like a hawk at the reception just now with my lip curled.

DORELIA: Watching what?

CECIL: The mourners. With elation shining in their eyes, induced by cold red wine, washed down with damp digestive biscuits.

DORELIA: (*Almost smiling.*) What a tribute to the caterer!

CECIL: Do you know why they look elated, Dodo?

DORELIA: Tell me.

CECIL: Because they had just experienced the thrill of being close to death without being required to suffer from its sting in person.

DORELIA: You're being naughty again, Cecil.

CECIL: I'm trying to cheer you up.

DORELIA: It's too soon, Cecil. Thank you all the same.

CECIL: You're a brave girl, Dodo. Well, I must be going. (*He goes to kiss her.*) Good-night, Dodo. I'll ring you in the morning.

He goes towards the door and turns when he gets half-way to see her sitting staring ahead.

Did you see the gypsy in the graveyard?

DORELIA: (*Snapping back into the present.*) Which one?

CECIL: The one next to me. He picked a rose out of the hedge and threw it into the grave.

DORELIA: Yes. I did see that.

CECIL: And did you hear him say, "A wild rose from a wild man"?

DORELIA: No.

CECIL: I did. His face was wet with tears.

He pauses, noting that this pleases her and moves on to the door and turns again.

Of course, he could have said with equal truth "A wild rose from a wild man to another wild man", couldn't he? (*He makes to leave.*)

DORELIA: He called me Ida by mistake – remember – the last day you sat for him.

CECIL stops and turns.

CECIL: That's what I meant.

DORELIA: It made me terribly unhappy.

CECIL: So I saw. You ran out of the room.

DORELIA: Then I remembered Ida used to tell me that he often called her Dodo after he'd had a few. (*She looks up with a smile.*) It made me feel much better, bless her.

CECIL goes.

DORELIA sits a while. Then she gets up and goes round the studio looking at the various pictures. Finally she goes, after looking back as though for the last time.

CURTAIN.